DEADLY DISEASES AND EPIDEMICS

TYPHOID FEVER

DEADLY DISEASES AND EPIDEMICS

TYPHOID FEVER

Donald Emmeluth

CONSULTING EDITOR
I. Edward Alcamo
Distinguished Teaching Professor of Microbiology,
SUNY Farmingdale

FOREWORD BY
David Heymann
World Health Organization

CHELSEA HOUSE
P U B L I S H E R S
An imprint of Infobase Publishing

Dedication
We dedicate the books in the DEADLY DISEASES AND EPIDEMICS series to Ed Alcamo, whose wit, charm, intelligence, and commitment to biology education were second to none.

Typhoid Fever

Copyright © 2004 by Infobase Publishing

Chelsea House
An imprint of Infobase Publishing
132 West 31st Street
New York NY 10001

Library of Congress Cataloging-in-Publication Data
Emmeluth, Donald.
    Typhoid fever/by Donald Emmeluth.
        p. cm.—(Deadly diseases and epidemics)
Includes bibliographical references and index.
Contents: Historical overview—Causes of typhoid fever—Who came to lunch!—I've got a fever: is it typhoid?—Treating typhoid fever—Preventing typhoid fever—The problems of antibiotic resistance—Future concerns—Hopes for the future.
    ISBN 0-7910-7464-1
    1. Typhoid fever—Juvenile literature. [1. Typhoid fever. 2. Diseases.]
I. Title. II. Series.
RC187.E57 2003
616.9'272—dc22   2003016577

Chelsea House books are available at special discounts when purchased in bulk quantities for businesses, associations, institutions, or sales promotions. Please call our Special Sales Department in New York at (212) 967-8800 or (800) 322-8755.

You can find Chelsea House on the World Wide Web at http://www.chelseahouse.com

Series design by Terry Mallon
Cover design by Keith Trego

Printed in the United States of America

Bang 21C 10 9 8 7 6 5 4 3 2

This book is printed on acid-free paper.

Table of Contents

Foreword

In the 1960s, infectious diseases—which had terrorized generations—were tamed. Building on a century of discoveries, the leading killers of Americans both young and old were being prevented with new vaccines or cured with new medicines. The risk of death from pneumonia, tuberculosis, meningitis, influenza, whooping cough, and diphtheria declined dramatically. New vaccines lifted the fear that summer would bring polio, and a global campaign was approaching the global eradication of smallpox. New pesticides like DDT cleared mosquitoes from homes and fields, thus reducing the incidence of malaria which was present in the southern United States and a leading killer of children worldwide. New technologies produced safe drinking water and removed the risk of cholera and other water-borne diseases. Science seemed unstoppable. Disease seemed destined to almost disappear.

But the euphoria of the 1960s has evaporated.

Microbes fight back. Those causing diseases like TB and malaria evolved resistance to cheap and effective drugs. The mosquito evolved the ability to defuse pesticides. New diseases emerged, including AIDS, Legionnaires, and Lyme disease. And diseases which have not been seen in decades re-emerge, as the hantavirus did in the Navajo Nation in 1993. Technology itself actually created new health risks. The global transportation network, for example, meant that diseases like West Nile virus could spread beyond isolated regions in distant countries and quickly become global threats. Even modern public health protections sometimes failed, as they did in Milwaukee, Wisconsin in 1993 which resulted in 400,000 cases of the digestive system illness cryptosporidiosis. And, more recently, the threat from smallpox, a disease completely eradicated, has returned along with other potential bioterrorism weapons such as anthrax.

The lesson is that the fight against infectious diseases will never end.

In this constant struggle against disease, we as individuals have a weapon that does not require vaccines or drugs, the warehouse of knowledge. We learn from the history of science that "modern" beliefs can be wrong. In this series of books, for example, you will learn that diseases like syphilis were once thought to be caused by eating potatoes. The invention of the microscope set science on the right path. There are more positive lessons from history. For example, smallpox was eliminated by vaccinating everyone who had come in contact with an infected person. This "ring" approach to controlling smallpox is still the preferred method for confronting a smallpox outbreak should the disease be intentionally reintroduced.

At the same time, we are constantly adding new drugs, new vaccines, and new information to the warehouse. Recently, the entire human genome was decoded. So too was the genome of the parasite that causes malaria. Perhaps by looking at the microbe and the victim through the lens of genetics we will to be able to discover new ways of fighting malaria, still the leading killer of children in many countries.

Because of the knowledge gained about such diseases as AIDS, entire new classes of anti-retroviral drugs have been developed. But resistance to all these drugs has already been detected, so we know that AIDS drug development must continue.

Education, experimentation, and the discoveries which grow out of them are the best tools to protect health. Opening this book may put you on the path of discovery. I hope so, because new vaccines, new antibiotics, new technologies and, most importantly, new scientists are needed now more than ever if we are to remain on the winning side of this struggle with microbes.

David Heymann
Executive Director
Communicable Diseases Section
World Health Organization
Geneva, Switzerland

1

Historical Overview

No one knows when typhoid fever first appeared. When Hippocrates described symptoms that included a fever, he was probably offering one of the first recorded descriptions of typhoid fever. When Emperor Augustus fell ill with typhoid fever, Roman physician Antonius Musa treated him with cold baths; this was the best treatment ancient doctors could provide without a more thorough understanding of this ailment.

While Alexander the Great conquered the world, he, in turn, was probably conquered by an unseen microbe. Plutarch's description of Alexander's symptoms leaves little doubt that Alexander probably died of typhoid fever in A.D. 323.

TYPHOID VS. TYPHUS—A FEVERISH PROBLEM

In 1659, Thomas Willis accurately described typhoid fever based solely on clinical observations. A number of additional accurate descriptions of typhoid fever were offered in the 1800s, but it is the work of William Gerhard in 1837 that clearly distinguishes between typhoid and typhus fevers, based solely on clinical differences between these two ailments. Unfortunately, critics continued to believe the two diseases were in fact the same. Karl J. Erberth is credited with isolating the bacterium responsible for typhoid fever in 1880. Once the bacterium was identified, diagnosis of typhoid became much easier.

Typhoid fever and typhus both cause high fevers, but their other symptoms are quite different. Typhus is spread by lice while typhoid fever is spread when water or food are contaminated by fecal matter. Symptoms of typhus include a large dark red rash that begins on the trunk of the body and moves to the extremities. Patients usually have a very high fever that may reach 104°F. As the temperature persists the patient tends to become delirious and hallucinate. Permanent damage to the heart and blood vessels is also a common result.

OBSERVATIONS AND DISEASE

In 1850, Sir Edward Jenner (Figure 1.1) used clinical symptoms and the post-mortem appearance of victims to distinguish typhoid fever from typhus. Jenner is perhaps best known for having developed the first vaccine against smallpox. Using fluid from the lesions of a common disorder known as cowpox, Jenner prepared a solution containing the infected fluid and injected it into a young boy. Jenner had noted that the subject from whom he had collected the cowpox-infected fluid (a milkmaid) had never gotten smallpox; thus, he hypothesized that the boy would be protected from the ravages of smallpox, too.

Jenner's observations were correct. We now know that cowpox and smallpox are members of the same family of viruses, and the body cannot distinguish between them. Antibodies produced against cowpox viruses will also protect against smallpox viruses. Jenner is credited with the development of the first vaccine. The word vaccine is derived from the latin *vacca* which means cow, the source of the material Jenner used.

Figure 1.1 *Edward Jenner, pictured here, was the first to experiment with vaccines. He hypothesized that transferring some of the **pus** from a cowpox lesion to a healthy person might induce immunity to smallpox. We now know that vaccines cause the body to produce antibodies, which help to ward off serious illnesses.*

Typhoid fever has greatly affected modern American life. Researchers developing the history of Jamestown, Virginia, believe that typhoid fever may have killed more than 6,000 settlers between 1607 and 1624. In the 1800s, United States Presidents Grover Cleveland and William Howard Taft both contracted and recovered from typhoid fever in their youth. One president was not so fortunate. President Zachary Taylor attended a July 4th celebration in Washington, D.C., in 1850. The day was hot and the ice-chilled cherries were tasty. The ice, unfortunately, was contaminated with the microorganism that causes typhoid fever. Taylor contracted the disease and died on July 9, 1850.

TYPHOID'S MOST FAMOUS CARRIER

Whatever the early history, one name will always be linked with this disease. It is said that everyone will have 15 minutes of fame during his or her lifetime, but Mary Mallon has endured nearly 100 years of infamy. She was known as "Typhoid Mary" (Figure 1.2).

Mary came to the United States from Ireland in 1883 and earned a living by working as a cook. On August 4, 1906, Mary began working for the Charles Warren family. A wealthy New York banker, Warren had rented a house on the north shore of Long Island in a well-to-do area known as Oyster Bay. Mary's desserts were quite popular, but unfortunately, they often contained a few unseen extras, namely typhoid bacteria. From August 27 to September 3 of that year, six of the 11 people in the house contracted typhoid fever. Typhoid fever was an unusual occurrence in Oyster Bay, and investigators could not find its cause.

Mr. and Mrs. George Thompson, who owned the house that Mr. Warren had rented, became concerned that they would not be able to rent the house again. They hired a sanitary engineer named George Soper to find the source of the outbreak. By this time, Mary had stopped working for the Warrens,

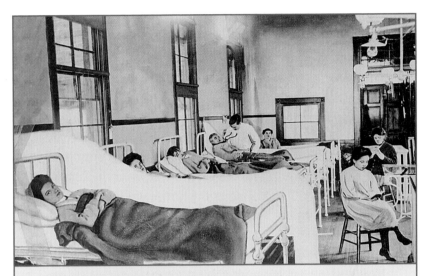

Figure 1.2 Mary Mallon was the most infamous carrier of typhoid fever and gained the nickname "Typhoid Mary." She was immune to the disease, but continued to pass it on to other people while working as a cook in New York City and its surrounding areas. She was instructed to find a new career, but she did not, and was eventually isolated on North Brother Island (shown here) where she lived until she died.

fearing that she, too, would contract the fever. After ruling out several other possibilities, Soper became convinced that Mary was a healthy **carrier** of the disease. Soper was the first person to identify a healthy typhoid carrier in the United States.

At this point, Mary was now working as a cook in a Park Avenue home in Manhattan. Soper tracked her down and told her that her cooking was spreading disease and killing people. He demanded samples of her feces, urine, and blood for testing. Mary disagreed, grabbed a kitchen knife, and chased Soper down the hallway.

Having survived this encounter with Mary, Soper began to look at Mary's work history for the previous ten years. She had worked for eight families. Seven of those families, including her current employer on Park Avenue, had contracted typhoid fever. A total of 22 people had become infected and one had died.

Soper's data convinced the New York City health inspector that Mary was a carrier of typhoid fever, and in March 1907 Mary was arrested and her feces, blood, and urine were tested for the typhoid **bacillus**. Her feces showed such high concentrations of the typhoid bacterium that some commented she was a "living culture tube." She was moved to an isolated cottage on the grounds of the Riverside Hospital, located on North Brother Island between the Bronx and Rikers Island. She remained there for three years and gained the title of "Typhoid Mary" at that time.

Mary continued to insist she had always been healthy and never had typhoid fever. She felt that it was unfair that she was forced to live in isolation. Her plight was written about in the local New York newspapers and soon the public was also asking why the government was picking on this woman. Public health officials in New York were usually willing to allow disease carriers to leave as long as they did not work in jobs where they handled or served food.

After three years in Riverside Hospital, Mary was freed on the conditions that she remain in touch with the health department and not work anywhere where she would be in contact with food. Unable to earn a living from washing clothes, she dropped from public view in 1915. A few months later, a number of typhoid cases occurred at Sloane Maternity Hospital in Manhattan. It appeared that Mary had broken her promise and was once again handling and serving food. Using the alias of "Mrs. Brown," she served as a cook and infected 25 doctors, nurses, and staff. Two died. She was caught and returned to North Brother Island, where she lived out the rest of her life, 23 years, in a one-room cottage. When she died in 1938, there were 237 other typhoid carriers living under health department observation, some on the island and others at their homes.

While Mary Mallon was certainly the best-known individual to be a typhoid carrier, she was not the most lethal. A man named Tony Labella caused more than 120 cases of typhoid fever, resulting in seven deaths. He was allowed to work as a laborer as long as he met with health officials weekly. Alphonse Cotils was another healthy carrier who was caught working with food after being told of his infectious status. An owner of a restaurant and bakery, Cotils was allowed to go free when he promised to conduct his business by telephone. Both LaBella and Cotils lived at the same time as Mary Mallon but received much less notice.

The typhoid fever bacterium does not respect gender, age, or geographic region. Wilbur Wright, co-inventor of the airplane, died of typhoid fever in 1912. In 1923, a woman in Salt Lake City, Utah, became ill with what was diagnosed as "walking typhoid." Although weak from her illness, she continued to work in a delicatessen. At least 188 cases of typhoid fever, including 13 deaths, can be traced directly to this woman. Her name is not even recorded for posterity.

LINKING TYPHOID FEVER TO FOOD AND WATER

In the nineteenth century, doctors saw more cases of typhoid fever than almost any other disease. Many people recognized the link between this disease and contaminated food or beverages. However, there was no organized effort to educate the public or take action until local health boards were developed in the late 1800s.

Typhoid fever remains a common problem in undeveloped countries even today, but we have known that it is spread by contaminated food and water since the 1800s. In England in 1873, William Budd showed that fecal contamination of drinking water was a major way of spreading typhoid fever. Such contamination was a common problem in overcrowded cities that had no adequate sewage system. The death in 1859 of the English Prince Albert from typhoid fever served as a stimulus to improve sewage systems in the major English cities and provide public health information to the general population.

The problem was no less acute in the United States. In the late 1800s, Chicago developed a unique strategy to clean up its water supply (see box below).

FIGHTING TYPHOID FEVER WITH SCIENCE

By 1896, Almroth E. Wright in England and Richard Pfeiffer and Wilhelm Kolle in Germany had developed a typhoid **vaccine** for humans. When injected into guinea pigs, heat-killed bacteria caused the animals to produce proteins (**antibodies**) that protected guinea pigs from getting the disease when they were injected with typhoid bacteria.

NO PROBLEM–JUST REVERSE THE FLOW OF THE RIVER

The original water system for Chicago was developed in 1842. As the city grew, the water system became inadequate and contamination became more prevalent. The Chicago River had become an open cesspool as waste from homes and slaughterhouses flowed into it. After a heavy rain, the river would overflow into Lake Michigan, which was the source of the city's drinking water. By 1891, the typhoid fever death rate was over 17%.

The Metropolitan Sanitary District of Greater Chicago began operation in 1889. It had become clear that wastes had to be kept out of the water supply. To meet this goal, the city proposed to reverse the flow of the Chicago River and, thus, carry wastes away from the lake. To achieve this reversal of flow, the city built a canal and a series of artificial rivers over a period of 25 years. Today there are over 71 miles of canals, channels, and rivers that make up Chicago's waterway system. In 1955, the Metropolitan Sanitary District of Chicago was selected as one of the seven engineering wonders of the United States by the American Society of Civil Engineers.

The original vaccine produced a number of adverse reactions but was shown to be effective. Wright was able to vaccinate about 14,000 volunteers among the troops leaving for the Boer War in South Africa in 1899 (the armed conflict between Britain and the two Boer republics of South Africa). Unfortunately, those opposed to the vaccinations threw the vaccine cargo overboard. More than 58,000 cases of typhoid fever were reported among Indian soldiers, causing more than 9,000 deaths. Fortunately, by the end of WWI, the typhoid vaccine had become nearly routine within the British Army.

Typhoid fever was the major killer in the Spanish-American War of 1898. Dr. Walter Reed did magnificent work showing how the typhoid fever bacteria were spread during wartime. In 1900, Reed would become famous for discovering that the virus that causes yellow fever was carried by a mosquito. Therefore, eradication of the mosquito populations would eliminate the yellow fever scourge. His work on typhoid fever had a tremendous impact on military medicine. However, military culture of the day decreed that medical officers could only recommend, while line officers command. This led to medical officers being ignored by their military superiors, who were more concerned with their own problems.

Lacking the direction and cooperation of the military commanders, troops ignored medical advice and consequently contracted and spread the disease. Without cooperation, tension arose between medical officers and line officers, with tragic consequences for the health of American soldiers. Dr. Reed's work showed the importance of sanitation in preventing and spreading the disease. More than anything else, it showed that different divisions of the military, (line officers and medical officers) had to work together to prevent the spread of this deadly disease. A number of important developments came from the discoveries of that time, among them the establishment of a Department of Military

Hygiene at the United States Military Academy at West Point and mandatory vaccinations against typhoid fever.

By the late 1800s, knowledge about the cause of typhoid fever and how to prevent it was well established. George Widal reported that he had developed a diagnostic test for typhoid fever using the **serum** of patients who were recovering from the disease. However, a cure for the disease would need to wait for the discovery and development of **antibiotics.**

In 1947, the antibiotic chloramphenicol was discovered. It was the type of antibiotic that would work against both of the major groups of bacteria. These two major groups are known as the gram-positive and the gram-negative bacteria. The designation refers to a type of staining technique developed by Hans Christian Gram in the 1800s. Due to certain properties of their cell membranes, bacteria develop a specific color reaction to the staining technique. Gram-positive bacteria turn purple in color while gram-negative bacteria become pinkish-red (the Gram stain procedure is further described in Chapter 2). Antibiotics that are effective against both gram-positive and gram-negative bacteria are known as broad-spectrum antibiotics. This newly discovered broad-spectrum antibiotic worked well against the typhoid bacterium and reduced death rates from about 12% to 2–3%. Dr. Joseph E. Smadel was the first to demonstrate the effective use of chloramphenicol against typhoid fever and various other diseases of the day. Unfortunately, this antibiotic also can cause blood disorders in some people.

In later chapters you will learn that this disease is still a problem worldwide. Our understanding of how it is spread and, thus, how easily it can be stopped stands in stark contrast to its continued existence. New and more effective vaccines and antibiotics are being developed. Our understanding of how typhoid bacteria cause disease symptoms at the cellular and molecular level is expanding. Hopes for its complete eradication are increasing but are also tied to economic and demographic factors that currently deprive people in developing countries of clean food and water, sanitary sewage treatment, and safe food-handling practices.

2

Causes of Typhoid Fever

When seven or eight members of the McCrary family in Caldwell County, Missouri, died in 1835, their illness was simply called "McCrary's Fever." Caldwell County continued to suffer through a number of **epidemics** over the next 50 years. Cemetery markers attest to the large number of children who died during that period. When typhoid fever, now recognized by name, came again to Caldwell County in 1874, people thought that it was caused by some poison that came from fresh virgin soil that had been dug up recently by shovel or plow, or from the dry prairie grasses. We now know that this persistent disease is caused by common bacteria.

SALMONELLA AND ITS IRRITATING FAMILY

When the microorganism responsible for typhoid fever was isolated in 1880 by Karl J. Erberth, doctors were finally able to diagnose typhoid fever and distinguish it from several diseases with similar symptoms accurately. Typhoid fever is caused by a bacterium known as *Salmonella typhi*. This family of bacteria, *Salmonella*, is named after Daniel E. Salmon, an American veterinarian, who first described the micro-organism in 1885. You will learn more about the naming of bacteria later in this chapter.

Before we learn more about the specific bacteria that cause typhoid fever, we need to learn a little about bacteria in general. Figure 2.1 shows the relationships between *Salmonella* and other closely related bacteria and lists some of the diseases they cause.

The *Salmonella* organisms belong to the family Enterobacteriaceae that includes the genus *Shigella*, the genus *Escherichia*, and the genus *Vibrio*. All of these genera contain species that inhabit and may

18

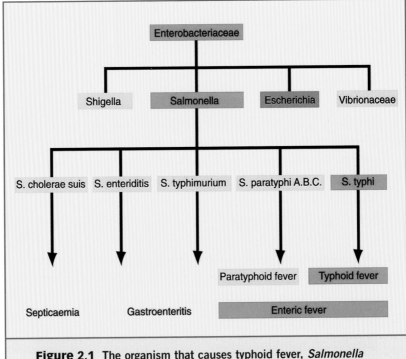

Figure 2.1 The organism that causes typhoid fever, *Salmonella typhi*, is part of a larger group of *Salmonella* bacteria. The different types of *Salmonella*, all of which are part of the family Enterobacteriaceae, are shown in this diagram.

inflame or irritate the intestines, causing intestinal infections and diarrhea in humans. The genus *Salmonella* contains a number of species known to cause symptoms ranging from discomfort to death.

More than 107 different strains of the typhoid bacteria have been identified, although there are more than 2,200 strains of *Salmonella enterica*. **Strains** are variations of a species that react differently to specific nutrients or, in some cases, to specific antibiotics. A **serotype** is a strain that has a unique surface molecule that may cause production of specific antibodies. Those antibodies may bind to that strain but not to other strains of the same species.

WHAT ARE BACTERIA?

Living things on this planet are currently placed into five large categories called Kingdoms. There is the Plant Kingdom, Animal Kingdom, Fungi Kingdom, Protista Kingdom, and Bacteria (or Prokaryote) Kingdom.

The cells of all living organisms are organized in one of two ways. Cells from the Plant, Animal, Fungi, and Protista kingdoms all contain compartments constructed from internal cellular membranes. These compartments, which help to separate chemicals and other materials from the interior of the cell, are called **organelles**, or miniature organs. Organelles include the nucleus, lysosomes, and the mitochondria. This type of cellular organization, with clearly defined and identifiable organelles, is described as the **eukaryotic** type of cellular organization. The term eukaryotic means "true nucleus" and comes

SALMONELLA BACTERIA GET A NEW NAME

In the late 1990s, a new naming scheme for the *Salmonella* bacteria was proposed. This new nomenclature, or naming system, is based on **DNA relatedness**. This new system would recognize only two species: *Salmonella bongori* and *Salmonella enterica* (both the genus and species names are italicized). All human pathogens would be regarded as **serovars** within subspecies I of *Salmonella enterica*. The proposed nomenclature would change *Salmonella typhi* to *Salmonella enterica* serovar Typhi, abbreviated *S*. Typhi (note that Typhi is not italicized and a capital letter is used). Some official agencies have adopted the new nomenclature. However, most articles and books, including this one, will continue to use the name of *Salmonella typhi*.

The term serovar is now used in place of the term serotype. It refers to a serological variety of a species characterized by its ability to induce antibody formation.

from the Greek *eu* meaning "proper," "good," or "true," and *karyon* meaning nucleus. Therefore, cells of plants, animals, fungi, and protozoa are known as eukaryotic cells or eukaryotes because of their internal cellular organization.

The Bacteria, or Prokaryote, kingdom includes cells with a different type of internal organization. Bacterial cells lack membrane-defined organelles, are normally smaller than eukaryotic cells, and have few clearly defined internal structures. Because bacteria lack organelles such as the nucleus, they are described as being **prokaryotic** cells. *Pro* is Greek for "before" and *karyon* refers to the nucleus. Because bacterial cells do not have a nucleus, the genetic information (a single circular DNA molecule) resides in the cell with no membrane structure surrounding it. This type of cellular organization has served bacteria well for over 3.5 billion years.

IMPORTANT BACTERIAL STRUCTURES

Bacteria were originally classified as very small plants because, like plants, they have a cell wall protecting their cell membranes and the interior of the cell. However, bacterial cell walls are made of molecules that are different from the molecules in plant cell walls. Bacterial cell walls are made of a molecule called *peptidoglycan,* which contains amino acids (the building blocks of proteins (*peptido*), and carbohydrates, which include simple sugars like glucose *(glycan).* This unique molecule is not found among eukaryotes (including humans), so the human immune system tries to remove or destroy it.

Different groups of bacteria have differing amounts of peptidoglycan in their cell walls. When treated with different dyes, these differences in the amount of peptidoglycan and other factors cause bacterial cells to retain or lose the color of specific dyes. One very famous and important staining reaction used to differentiate between bacteria is the Gram stain process. In this process, bacteria are treated with a series of different-colored dyes. If the bacteria retain the first dye color (crystal violet) throughout the entire staining procedure, they look purple at the end of the test. Such bacteria are called **gram-positive** bacteria. Other bacteria lose the first dye in the process and take on the color of the last dye (called the counterstain). These bacteria look pink or light red and are called **gram-negative** bacteria.

It is also important to know that bacteria can move on their own if they possess a structure called a flagellum. A flagellum (plural: flagella) helps the bacterium move toward areas where there is food and security and away from harmful areas. Flagella are made from a unique protein called flagellin. The human immune system does not recognize this protein so it works to kill it.

The unique molecular structures of bacterial cell walls and flagella will become important to our understanding of vaccines that can be used to prevent typhoid fever. The unique structure of the peptidoglycan molecule also makes it a target for antibiotics such as penicillin. Antibiotics have been very successful in killing the bacteria that cause illnesses like typhoid fever.

A THIRD FORM OF LIFE

Another group of microorganisms also has a prokaryotic type of cellular organization. They are called the Archaebacteria, or simply the Archae, and they resemble the bacteria in size and prokaryotic organization. However, the Archae are quite different genetically from both eukaryotic and prokaryotic types of cells. Archae contain genetic information similar to the eukaryotes and also genetic information similar to bacteria. In addition, more than 40 percent of their genetic information is totally unique, resembling neither eukaryotes nor bacteria. The Archae live in extreme environments, earning them the name "Extremophiles." Extreme environments might include the absence of oxygen (the term **anaerobic** describes an oxygen-free environment) or very high heat, such as inside volcanoes.

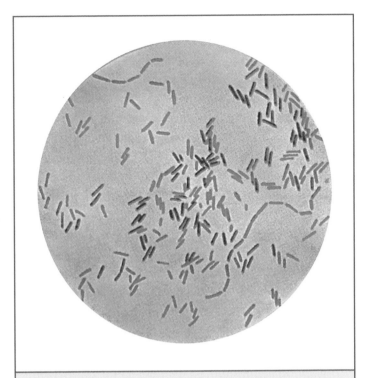

Figure 2.2 An electron micrograph of *Salmonella typhi* is shown here. The bacteria are gram-negative, so they appear red. The bacteria are classified as bacilli (bacillus, singular) meaning that they are rod-shaped.

THE TYPHOID BACTERIUM

Bacteria come in three basic shapes. Bacteria shaped like a rod or a pencil are known as *bacilli* (bacillus, singular). Bacteria shaped like a circle or a sphere are known as *cocci* (**coccus**, singular). Bacteria that are shaped like spirals or the letter "c," or are wound tightly like a spring are known as *spirilli* (*sprillum*, singular).

The bacterium responsible for typhoid fever is called *Salmonella typhi*. It is a rod-shaped bacillus, about 5 times longer than it is wide (Figure 2.2). It is **aerobic** (requires oxygen) and moves using multiple flagella.

The typhoid bacillus, like other members of its family, is gram-negative. The cell walls of gram-negative bacteria contain less peptidoglycan than those of gram-positive bacteria. The outermost layer of the cell wall of gram-negative bacteria also contains lipopolysaccharides (LPS) and proteins. Because LPS is toxic to mammals, it is called an **endotoxin**. When the bacterium dies, the LPS becomes free in the serum.

Blood is divided into the red and white blood cells and platelets known as the formed elements, and the fluid portion known as the plasma. When clotting factors, such as various proteins, are removed, the light yellow fluid that is left is known as the serum. The serum contains the immune proteins known as antibodies, and free LPS may interact with these antibodies causing a number of problems in humans, including fever, changing blood cell counts, and leaking blood vessels, which could lead to shock.

This outer layer, also called the outer membrane, has an inside and an outside. The outside of the membrane contains all the lipopolysaccharides. There are two parts to LPS—a molecule called Lipid A, which anchors to the membrane, and the polysaccharide chain that extends into the environment (Figure 2.3). Part of this polysaccharide chain is a series of repeating sugar units known as O antigen. The name is derived from the fact that the polysaccharide is exposed to the outer environment. Host defenses can hone in on these sugars; however, bacteria can change the makeup of the O antigen to confuse the human host's immune system.

The O antigens are involved in the production of the fever. O antigens are buried in the cell wall of the typhoid bacillus, and this makes them difficult to destroy with heat (so they are not damaged even when the host experiences high fever). The H antigen of the typhoid bacillus is the protein associated with the flagella. The Vi (virulence) antigen is a polysaccharide on the outside of the cell wall. This antigen makes it difficult for white blood cells to engulf the typhoid

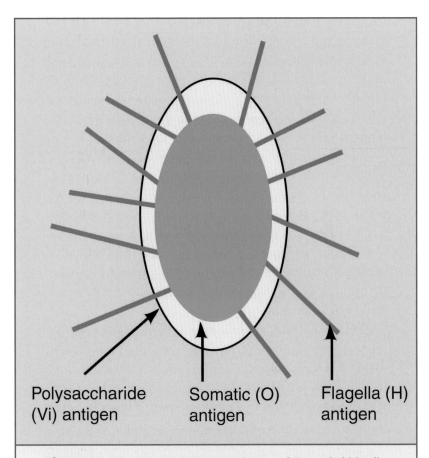

Polysaccharide
(Vi) antigen

Somatic (O)
antigen

Flagella (H)
antigen

Figure 2.3 The outer and inner membranes of the typhoid bacillus contain specific antigens. The O antigen, which is involved in the production of the fever, is located with the cell wall and thus is heat stable. The Vi antigen, which protects the bacillus from white blood cells, is easily destroyed by high temperatures—e.g., boiling—and is more exposed than the O antigen. Removal of the Vi antigen causes the immediate death of the organism. This shows the importance of boiling water and thoroughly cooking food as a way of destroying the bacteria.

bacillus. Its position on the outside of the cell membrane makes it vulnerable to heat. If the Vi antigen is destroyed, the typhoid bacillus will die.

TALES OF THE ELUSIVE TRAVELER

Typhoid fever is also known as **enteric** fever. The word "enteric" refers to the intestine. To cause disease, the bacteria must be swallowed. Once swallowed, the bacteria travel through the digestive tract and are engulfed by white blood cells called **mononuclear phagocytes**. The normal job of the phagocytes is to engulf and digest invading bacteria, fungal spores, and viruses. When large numbers of bacteria are ingested, many are able to bypass the phagocytes and get to the small intestine. Stomach acids usually kill ingested bacteria. However, people whose stomach acid is less effective than in healthy adults, including infants and the elderly, are at risk for contracting typhoid fever. Taking antacids, like Tums® or Rolaids®, or medications that reduce stomach acidity increases the person's chance of contracting the disease.

When typhoid bacteria are ingested with water, the water not only dilutes the stomach acid but also passes rapidly through the stomach. After the bacteria multiply for a short time in the duodenum, the first section of the small intestine, they enter the epithelial cells of the intestinal mucosa (lining). From here, they come into contact with a special type of tissue in the intestine. This tissue, the **lymphatic tissue**, is important in developing and aiding the immune system. **Phagocytosis** (engulfment of materials, Figure 2.4), occurs in the lymphatic areas, usually by a type of white blood cells called **neutrophils**. Neutrophils can ingest, but not digest, typhoid bacteria. The bacteria enter the circulatory system before spreading to the liver, spleen, and lymph nodes. Inside the liver, spleen, and lymph nodes, the bacteria divide and eventually spread via the lymphatic system and bloodstream to most other organs of the body. Once they have invaded these other cells, the bacteria produce a wide range of symptoms.

As noted earlier, some bacteria, including *Salmonella typhi*, resist digestion by phagocytes. The Vi antigen protects the bacteria from being broken down by **free radical oxygen**

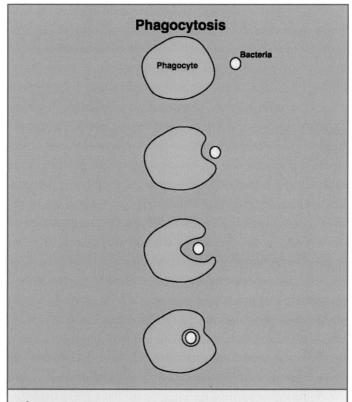

Figure 2.4 Phagocytosis (illustrated here) is a form of **endocytosis**, one of several methods the cell uses to bring in large and insoluble materials. The cell uses energy to extend its membrane around the invading bacterium or virus. The microbe is surrounded by the cell and becomes enclosed in a membrane within the cell. The cell then releases special enzymes that digest the microbe.

atoms. Bacteria multiply within the phagocytes during the normal 10 to 14-day incubation period of typhoid fever. The incubation period depends on the quantity of bacteria swallowed and varies from one to three weeks. As large numbers of bacteria start to fill an individual phagocyte, they begin to leak out of the cell and into the bloodstream, after which the symptoms associated with typhoid fever begin to appear.

When large numbers of bacteria are in the bloodstream, this condition is called **bacteremia**. The gallbladder and bile duct become infected, causing bacteria to be excreted with the bile, loading the intestinal tract with millions of bacteria and setting up a cycle of infection. In about 14% of infected people, the gallbladder is colonized with bacteria, but the patients have no symptoms of the disease. These people become carriers who can spread the disease.

In individuals who do not receive antibiotics, the bacteria cause a high fever that may persist for four to eight weeks. The gallbladder may respond to this invasion by becoming inflamed, a condition called **cholecystitis**. *Salmonella* may directly infect the gallbladder through the hepatic duct or spread to other areas of the body through the bloodstream.

The bacteria also invade the lymphatic tissue known as Peyer's Patches, which is embedded in the membrane material (called **mesentery**) holding the intestine together. Invasion of the intestine can lead to intestinal bleeding or an actual hole occurring in the wall of the intestine (called a perforation). As a result, intestinal contents may leak into the abdominal cavity. When the lining of the abdominal cavity is severely irritated or inflamed, a condition called **peritonitis** can result. Peritonitis is a frequent cause of death from typhoid fever. The liver and spleen may enlarge. If the enlargement is too great, the spleen may rupture. Intestinal bleeding leads to anemia, or low red blood cell count.

Full recovery from untreated typhoid fever may take several months. Typhoid fever is an enteric fever. It is a disease that begins as an infection of the digestive tract and develops into an illness that affects the entire body (called a systemic illness).

BACTERIA AND PERSONAL HYGIENE

The *Salmonella typhi* bacteria can be transferred from the urine and stool of infected people to any food or drink they may be serving or preparing. This pathway is sometimes called the **fecal-oral route** of disease transmission. When people who are carriers of the typhoid bacteria do not wash their hands thoroughly (or at all) after urination or defecation, they risk passing the organisms to others. In countries where open sewage is accessible to flies, the insects land on the sewage, pick up the bacteria, and then contaminate food that is later eaten by humans.

In regions of the world where sanitation, garbage disposal, and food hygiene are lacking, typhoid fever continues to destroy lives. The principal carrier, or vector, for typhoid bacteria is water. The infection is frequently transmitted by drinking or eating food that has been made with or washed in water contaminated with fecal matter. The disease can also be spread through crops that have been fertilized with human feces that are contaminated with typhoid bacteria. Humans are the only natural host for *Salmonella typhi*.

3

Guess Who Came to Lunch!

THE INVITATION

The letter Jim had hoped for finally showed up in his mailbox. He remembered that day clearly. The return address had the university logo and read "International Outreach Project." Jim opened the letter with trembling hands, which shook with joy as he read the introductory sentence: "We are pleased to inform you that you have been selected . . ." The rest of the words were a blur. All he cared about was that he was going to visit India.

Jim had been granted a scholarship that would allow him to observe the healthcare system of a major Indian urban center and its outlying villages. As a health systems administration major at the university, Jim had been studying health care systems in several countries. The opportunity to visit a country and observe its system up close and in person was a dream come true. Most of Jim's time in India would be spent at the All India Institute of Medical Sciences in New Delhi. He hoped he would also be able to visit the Department of Laboratory Medicine at the Institute.

PREPARING FOR THE TRIP

Jim had lots of things to do—get a passport and a visa, check on the type of clothing to wear, and read about local customs, just to name a few. The trip was planned for June and July. Jim would return home during the first week in August, about three weeks before the start of the fall semester. Jim's university provided him pre-departure information. In addition to making sure he was in good health and that his vaccinations were up to date, he needed to be vaccinated against several diseases. He would also need to prepare himself with information as to how to remain healthy while traveling abroad. Both the Centers for Disease Control and Prevention (CDC) and the World Health Organization (WHO) provide the public with useful information, including what vaccines are required and suggested for travel to various countries and what diseases are present in a particular area and how they are transmitted (Figure 3.1).

Jim also found that June was the beginning of the monsoon rainy season and July was the peak month for rainfall. Summer temperatures in India (June and July) range from an average of 34.5°C to a high of 47°C (approximately 95°F to 115°F).

THE ALL INDIA INSTITUTE

The All India Institute is considered a center of excellence for medical education and research in South and Central Asia, with fantastic facilities for teaching, research, and patient care. In addition to programs involving urban health services and geriatric care, staff working in the Community Medicine Center travel into the city and rural areas. Centralized "camps" are set up to provide local people with information on such health-related topics as alcoholism, family planning, mother and child care, drug addiction, and polio. These camps also provide immunizations against tuberculosis, measles, diphtheria, pertussis (whooping cough), and tetanus.

There are also a number of research projects where the Institute is working with researchers in other areas of the world, particularly Southeast Asia and parts of Africa. Dengue fever virus and antibiotic resistant strains of the tuberculosis bacterium are two of those collaborative projects. Altogether, the Institute conducts teaching and research in over 42 disciplines, and it runs a College of Nursing. The Institute's mission statement is "To bring together in one place educational facilities of the highest order for the training of the personnel in all important branches of the health activity."

Category	Vaccine
Routine Vaccination	Diphtheria/tetanus/pertussis (DPT) Hepatitis B (HBV) *Haemophilus influenzae* type b (Hib) Measles (MMR) Poliomyelitis (oral or inactivated vaccine)
Selective use for travelers	Cholera Influenza Hepatitis A (HAV) Japanese encephalitis Lyme disease Meningococcal meningitis Pneumococcal disease Rabies Tick-borne encephalitis Tuberculosis (BCG) Typhoid fever Yellow fever (for individual protection)
Mandatory vaccination	Yellow fever (for protection of vulnerable countries) Meningococcal meningitis (for Hajj, Umra)

Figure 3.1 Before visiting certain countries, travelers may need to be immunized against specific diseases. These vaccines are listed in this chart. Diptheria/tetanus/pertussis, Hepatitis B, **Haemophilus influenzae** type b, measles, and poliomyelitis are all vaccines that people in the United States should already have. Additional vaccines vary depending on the country the person will visit.

When Jim looked at these figures, he knew they also meant very high humidity and an increase in the fly population.

ARRIVING IN NEW DELHI

It was a clear day as Jim's plane headed into Indira Gandhi International Airport in New Delhi. He could see the Yamuna River and the high stone wall surrounding Delhi, which was built in 1638. The Yamuna River, a tributary of the Ganges, separates the old, crowded Delhi from the new, more spacious New Delhi. New Delhi is the capital of India and its third largest city. More than 11 million people are crowded into a city originally designed for 600,000. Urban sprawl is obvious

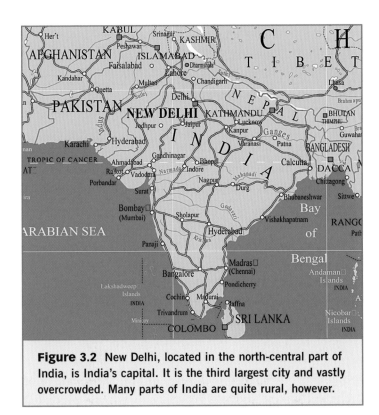

Figure 3.2 New Delhi, located in the north-central part of India, is India's capital. It is the third largest city and vastly overcrowded. Many parts of India are quite rural, however.

everywhere. Jim was prepared to see the large number of cows roaming the streets but was not prepared to see the troops of rhesus monkeys that had taken over some of the buildings in this cosmopolitan city (Figure 3.2).

After arriving at his hotel and getting settled in, Jim met with other students who were part of the project. The orientation session was designed to welcome and acquaint the students with each other, the city, and the Institute. The list of precautions that was also provided at the orientation was intended to keep the students healthy. They were told to stay hydrated, but to drink only bottled water, as tap water might be contaminated. All foods should be thoroughly cooked to kill bacteria, and the students should avoid eating food from street vendors, as it might contain harmful bacteria. They should not eat dairy food unless they were sure it had been pasteurized. The students should avoid playing with or touching animals as they might transmit diseases such as rabies and the plague. Lastly, if they were to go swimming, they should swim only in saltwater, as it tends to be safer than freshwater.

WORKING AT THE INSTITUTE

In the weeks that followed, Jim learned about the history of the city and the country. He found it necessary to adopt the habit of dousing himself with mosquito repellant to avoid being bitten by mosquitoes that might be carrying the malaria or yellow fever **parasites**.

Jim was amazed by what he saw, heard, and learned at the Institute. Working with the faculty members at the Center for Community Medicine, he found that they were constantly traveling and giving lectures at conferences worldwide. The scope of their research was impressive. They were studying many different health problems, including malnutrition in urban slum children 1 to 3 years of age, the presence of bronchial asthma in these groups, how parents perceived health problems, and if they sought treatment. They also looked at the prevalence of tooth cavities and dental abnormalities in people from rural areas and studied the pattern of traffic accidents in South Delhi. They also maintained a long-term study on the prevalence of typhoid fever.

Typhoid fever is **endemic** in India. One professor at the Community Medicine Center told Jim there are more than 3 million cases of typhoid fever reported each year. Death rates due to typhoid fever are between 1–2.5%. Children between the ages of 8 and 13 seem to have the highest attack rates, but children from 1 to 5 are also susceptible.

HOMEWARD BOUND

Jim's last week in India was extremely hectic. Jim and several other students spent two days at an outlying village helping to oversee the vaccination of young children. Their jobs were mainly administrative, taking care of the paperwork and meeting family members. One of the families even brought sandwiches for the students to eat. It would have been an insult to turn down the gift of food from people who did not have much to start with. Jim dutifully ate the sandwich amid a thick cloud of flies. The amount of flies had greatly increased during that last week since there had been a great deal of rain.

As much as Jim wanted to stay and learn more, it was time for him to head home. The time he had spent in India at the Institute would provide him with valuable insights that he could apply in his major of health systems administration. He began to understand the problems associated with health care in regions of the world that lack the infrastructure found in the more developed countries. He would never forget the abject poverty he had seen, but he would be happy to forget the high humidity, flies, and unsavory aromas he found in the slum camps. He knew that he wanted to come back and spend more time at the Institute.

After Jim had been home for a little more than a week, he began to feel ill, but he was not particularly worried. The tiredness he felt could probably be attributed to the hectic schedule he had been keeping and the long trip home. However, the headache, fever, and chills that began to occur more frequently as each day passed were distressing. The fever and chills did not occur with any regularity, so malaria could probably be ruled out as the cause. Jim felt some tenderness and pain in his abdominal area, his throat was inflamed, and he was constipated. He tried to determine what could be causing these symptoms. A limited number of possibilities began to emerge as likely causes of his discomfort, with typhoid fever at the top of his list. Jim recalled that 80% of the typhoid fever cases in the United States were brought back by travelers who had visited African or Asian countries. He never thought he could be one of those statistics.

4

I've Got a Fever. Is it Typhoid?

As much as he tried to avoid it, Jim knew he had to get to the doctor. His temperature was steadily climbing, and it was becoming clear that he had brought back some unwanted bacterial company. It seemed most likely that the culprit was the organism responsible for typhoid fever.

VISITING THE DOCTOR

Jim's family doctor had known Jim since he was a kid. In his career, the doctor had visited India, as well as such Southeast Asian countries as Indonesia, Cambodia, and Vietnam. He worked to raise community medical standards and improve living conditions in these countries. Consequently, Jim's doctor knew a great deal about tropical diseases common in these countries.

Once at his doctor's office, Jim provided a complete history of where he had been and what he had been doing over the last two months, especially during his last weeks in India. Jim also mentioned his suspicion that he might have typhoid fever. The doctor explained that if Jim did indeed have typhoid fever, the local health department must be informed.

PROCEDURES TO FOLLOW

Typhoid fever is classified as a reportable disease, specifically a Notifiable Bacterial Foodborne Disease or Condition. The Centers for Disease Control and Prevention and the Council of State and Territorial Epidemiologists work together to determine which diseases are reportable nationally. Information about disease outbreaks is sent from the local to the state health officials. State officials investigate and then send the information to the Centers for Disease Control and Prevention (CDC). The CDC then compiles the information and makes it available to the public in the *Morbidity and Mortality Weekly Report*, a publication filled with information about all sorts of diseases throughout the United States and the world.

Jim found that the procedures that must be followed when dealing with a suspected case of typhoid fever got even more complex. Since 1962, laboratories that isolate *Salmonella* from humans must send the isolated organisms to the state public health laboratories. At the state labs, the organisms are serotyped (recall the discussion of serotypes in Chapter 2), thus providing information that is useful to the public in general but not necessarily to the individual patient. The information can be used to trace large-scale trends in food-borne diseases. These isolated organisms are also tested for anti-microbial resistance, and this data is added to information at the national level (Figure 4.1).

FINDING THE CULPRIT

Jim's doctor explained that before a diagnosis of typhoid fever is given, other diseases with similar symptoms and incubation times need to be eliminated from consideration. A common disease in travelers returning from Southeast Asia is malaria. Typhoid fever and malaria can coexist in a patient. Another disease that fits some of the symptoms is brucellosis, which is associated with unpasteurized milk or cheese. Hepatitis A also shares many of the symptoms but usually starts with diarrhea and dark urine. The key in the presumptive diagnosis of typhoid fever is the fever itself, which continues to rise.

The doctor told Jim that in cases such as his, it is important to take a history of the patient that is detailed and specific for the time period in question. This allows a doctor to use

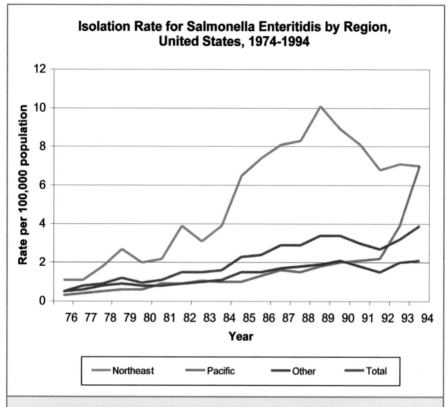

Isolation Rate for Salmonella Enteritidis by Region, United States, 1974-1994

Northeast — Pacific — Other — Total

Figure 4.1 When a person is suspected of having typhoid fever, the bacterium *Salmonella typhi* must be isolated from a blood sample to confirm the diagnosis. The Centers for Disease Control and Prevention keeps records of where in the United States the cases of typhoid fever occurred. In the late 1980s and early 1990s, the Northeast reported many more cases than any of the other three regions. Although the number of cases in the Pacific region spiked in 1993, it had not surpassed the Northeast by 1994.

clinical clues when examining the patient to narrow down the most likely diagnosis. Jim found that the activities he had been involved with in India provided ample opportunity for him to be exposed to the organism that causes malaria or the bacteria that causes typhoid fever.

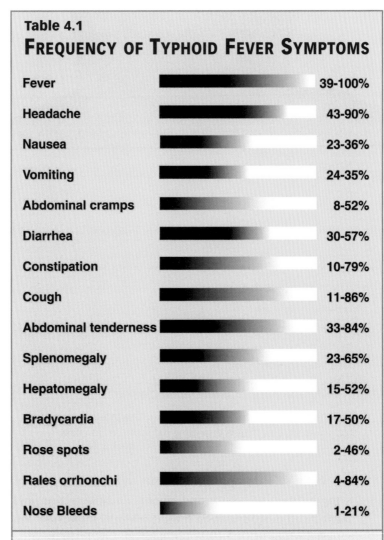

Table 4.1

FREQUENCY OF TYPHOID FEVER SYMPTOMS

Symptom	Frequency
Fever	39-100%
Headache	43-90%
Nausea	23-36%
Vomiting	24-35%
Abdominal cramps	8-52%
Diarrhea	30-57%
Constipation	10-79%
Cough	11-86%
Abdominal tenderness	33-84%
Splenomegaly	23-65%
Hepatomegaly	15-52%
Bradycardia	17-50%
Rose spots	2-46%
Rales orrhonchi	4-84%
Nose Bleeds	1-21%

Table 4.1 Fever, headaches, nausea, and vomiting are just some of the symptoms that a person with typhoid fever might experience. This table shows many of the symptoms and their frequency of occurrence. Fever is the most common symptom, occurring in up to 100% of the patients. Other symptoms are less likely to appear. For example, abdominal cramps may occur in anywhere from 8–52% of typhoid patients.

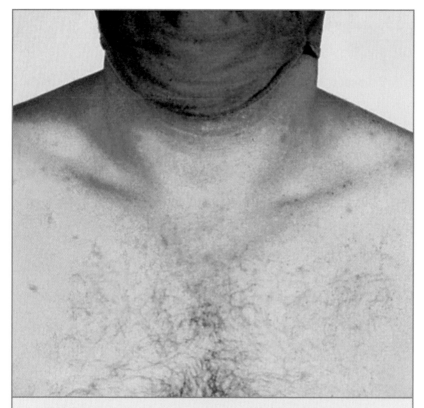

Figure 4.2 Red (or rose) spots are one characteristic symptom of typhoid fever. This man is displaying red spots on his chest.

Typhoid fever appears in many guises. The range of symptoms is impressive and varied. Early detection and identification of *Salmonella typhi* is critically important. Jim referred to the table shown on page 40, which shows what symptoms he might expect if it were confirmed that he was infected with the typhoid bacillus. This table (Table 4.1) gives the range of potential symptoms and their typical frequency for the disease. Figure 4.2 shows a man displaying **rose spots**, a characteristic of typhoid fever.

Initially, Jim felt like he might have the flu, but he was experiencing other symptoms that he knew were more serious.

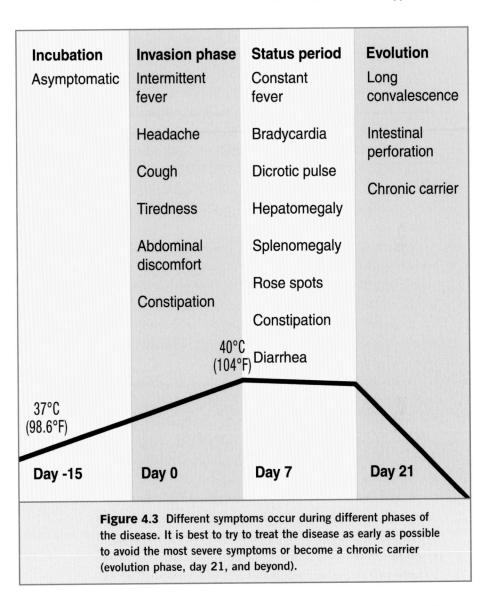

Incubation	Invasion phase	Status period	Evolution
Asymptomatic	Intermittent fever	Constant fever	Long convalescence
	Headache	Bradycardia	Intestinal perforation
	Cough	Dicrotic pulse	Chronic carrier
	Tiredness	Hepatomegaly	
	Abdominal discomfort	Splenomegaly	
	Constipation	Rose spots	
		Constipation	
		40°C (104°F) Diarrhea	

37°C (98.6°F)

| Day -15 | Day 0 | Day 7 | Day 21 |

Figure 4.3 Different symptoms occur during different phases of the disease. It is best to try to treat the disease as early as possible to avoid the most severe symptoms or become a chronic carrier (evolution phase, day 21, and beyond).

He noted with dismay that the constipation sometimes turned to diarrhea and that his temperature could reach 103°F. Fortunately, the long-term prognosis was good since he had seen the doctor early enough to avoid possible long-lasting damage to his internal systems (Figure 4.3).

Jim's background reading about typhoid fever pointed out that young adult male travelers under 30 years of age were most likely to develop typhoid fever. Consumption of food or beverages contaminated with feces is the most likely source of the infection. Flies spread the bacteria responsible for typhoid fever by landing on feces contaminated with the bacteria and then carrying the bacteria to foods, where they can multiply sufficiently to achieve an **infective dose**. An infective dose is the number of organisms required to cause the symptoms of the disease in an individual. It may vary from species to species.

Jim thought back to his last few days in India. He remembered the cloud of flies and mosquitoes in the urban slum areas. He also remembered the sandwiches provided by one of the families and the lettuce and fruit he had also eaten. He wondered if the water used for washing the fruit and irrigating the lettuce had been contaminated with typhoid bacteria.

As Jim would soon learn, a definitive diagnosis of *Salmonella typhi* is suggested by the presence of antibodies specific to the organism, antigens released from the organism, or the presence of *Salmonella* DNA in the body fluids. Isolation of the organism would confirm that diagnosis. Typically blood, bone marrow, feces, and urine are sampled.

Blood cultures are generally considered the best procedure for the definitive diagnosis of typhoid fever. About half of all patients will test positive within 72 hours. A culture of a bone marrow aspirate is considered the most sensitive test and will give positive culture rates of over 90%. Positive results are obtained from the bone marrow of patients even after antibiotic treatment has begun. *Salmonella typhi* has been isolated from cerebrospinal fluid, peritoneal fluid, lymph nodes located in the membrane attached to the loops of the intestine (mesentery), the pharynx, tonsils, and abscesses.

The Widal Test (Widal agglutination reaction) is a routine test used for serological diagnosis where technicians compare samples taken at two-week intervals. These samples are tested for changes in the concentration of specific proteins. Not all health care professionals are convinced of the reliability of this test since most strains of *Salmonella* share common proteins on their surfaces. Among the problems noted, they cite difficulties in producing uniform standards, which lead to unclear comparisons. In addition, there is the difficulty of interpreting test results from regions where the normal antibody concentration of the population already exposed to typhoid fever is unknown.

CULTURE METHODS

The bacteria responsible for typhoid fever are usually isolated from blood and bone marrow cultures only during the first two weeks of the illness. Stool (fecal) cultures are usually positive during the third to fifth weeks. Urine cultures are usually positive. Knowing whether the urine is positive is a useful way of knowing if this individual may become a chronic carrier.

When cultures from blood, feces, or urine are negative, cultures of liver biopsies or snippets from the rose spots on the skin may give positive results. Despite these general rules, the organism may be cultured from the stool at any time during the infection and may be cultured from the blood as late as the fifth week.

As Jim read about the diagnosis and treatment of typhoid fever, he found that the Department of Laboratory Medicine at the All India Institute of Medical Sciences in New Delhi had a great deal of experience identifying the bacteria that causes typhoid fever.

SEROLOGY

Tests designed to detect the presence of antibodies, which are produced when an animal is exposed to specific bacteria, have been used for many years. Most bacteria, *Salmonella* included, have a variety of proteins on their cell surfaces. When an animal's immune system detects the proteins, it starts to form antibodies that fight these proteins. In addition, the flagella of bacteria are made of a unique protein called flagellin, which is also detected by the body's immune system. Specific antibodies are produced in response to these flagellin proteins. These

LABORATORY IDENTIFICATION OF THE MICROORGANISM

Various types of growth materials are used in an attempt to grow bacteria. These materials, called media, contain various nutrients that will enhance the growth of the bacteria being sought. Sometimes inhibitory chemicals are added to the growth medium. They are designed to prevent the growth of microbes that might outgrow or overgrow the bacteria that are sought. Adding antibiotics to the growth materials would be an example. Conventional bile salt broth cultures give a positive culture in about two-thirds of the cases. Using streptokinase bile salt broth inoculated with minced blood clot increased the yield to over 90%. Streptokinase is an enzyme produced by certain streptococcal bacteria, which prevents the formation of blood clots.

A number of solid and liquid media can be used to isolate the *Salmonella typhi* organism. When relatively few bacteria are present in the stool, strontium selenite broth has shown to be superior to selenite F broth. S-S agar (*Salmonella-Shigella*) works better than XLD agar (xylose lysine deoxycholate) for isolation of *Salmonella typhi*, and bismuth sulfate agar is required if a carrier is being tested or if the likelihood of typhoid is high.

In addition, some biotechnology companies have developed high-speed culture methods that allow for proper identification of the organism.

proteins and other chemicals that induce antibody reactions are called **antigens**.

Typhoid bacteria possess antigens O, H, and Vi. The O antigen refers to proteins and other chemicals in the cell wall. The H antigen is found in the flagella. The Vi antigen is part of the capsule. The Vi antibody test is used to detect the presence of typhoid carriers. The Widal Test measures the concentration, or titer, of antibodies against the O and H antigens. Two samples are taken two weeks apart, and if there is a four-fold increase in the antibody titer, a finding of typhoid fever is suggested. However, the sensitivity and specificity of the Widal test varies from laboratory to laboratory. These variations in sensitivity, specificity, and predictive value seem to be caused by differences in techniques and patient populations, as well as cross reactivity of O and H antigens. At best, the results are suggestive rather than definitive. Another disadvantage of the Widal Test includes taking samples at 7–10-day intervals and comparing the increase in specific antibodies.

A dot **enzyme** immunoassay test was developed in the early 1990s that takes only 60 minutes and has been shown to be 95 percent sensitive. This test detects specific immunoglobulin M (**IgM**) and immunoglobulin G (**IgG**) antibodies and is commercially available. Other serological tests are used specifically to detect the presence of typhoid carriers.

NEW TESTING PROCEDURES

New testing procedures and older procedures used for different types of testing are now being used to detect *Salmonella typhi*. Indirect **hemagglutination** and indirect enzyme-linked immunosorbent assay (ELISA) for immunoglobulin M (IgM) and immunoglobulin G (IgG) antibodies to a polysaccharide produced by *Salmonella typhi* are some new test procedures being used. These tests can be used as screening tests to determine if the patient has been in contact with *Salmonella typhi*.

If the patient has been in contact with the organism or if the organism is still in his body, the immune system of the patient will produce antibodies specific for Salmonella or some of its surface molecules. The indirect hemagglutination test refers to the addition of specific antigens to the surface of the red blood cells used in the test procedure. If antibodies against that antigen are present, they will attach to the antigen and cause the red blood cells to clump (agglutinate). The indirect ELISA test is similar since it is also seeking the presence of antibodies against the bacteria or some of its molecules. In this case, polysaccharides (complex sugars) present on the surface of the bacteria serve as the antigen. The antigen is placed in shallow wells in a laboratory plate. Addition of blood to the wells allows the investigator to see if any clotting occurs, suggesting the presence of antibodies against those polysaccharides. The indirect fluorescent Vi antibody test is used to test for carriers. If the ELISA test is positive, the indirect fluorescent Vi antibody test may be used to confirm the results. A fluorescent dye is added to the Vi antigen and mixed with the patient's blood. If antibodies against the Vi antigen are present, they will combine with the antigen, and the dye and will glow when light of a specific wavelength is applied. They can be seen through a fluorescent microscope.

Monoclonal antibodies against flagellin protein are being developed. DNA probes have also been developed that can identify *Salmonella typhi* directly from blood and from isolated organisms taken from bacterial cultures. Detection was useful for suspected cases of typhoid fever. Blood tests confirmed 20 out of 20 culture positive cases and detected 12 out of 20 cases that had been determined to be negative by conventional means.

Jim's doctor gave him a prescription for an antibiotic and told him he would call with a definitive diagnosis as soon as he knew. Jim was not surprised when, three days later, the doctor called and told him he would soon be famous. He would make the next issue of the *Morbidity and Mortality Weekly Report*. Jim's samples had come back positive and showed he was infected with the typhoid bacillus. Jim was infected with a multidrug-resistant strain of the bacteria, so he went to see the doctor the next day to have the type and dosage of antibiotic adjusted. Jim was about to learn all about how antibiotics are used to treat disease.

5

Treating Typhoid Fever

Multidrug-resistant strains of *Salmonella typhi* have been identified in and around India since 1987. These strains are resistant to the major antibiotics used to treat typhoid fever—ampicillin or amoxicillin, chloramphenical, tetracycline, and co-trimoxazole. According to the CDC, *Salmonella typhi* kills over 600,000 people each year worldwide. Between 10 and 17 million cases of typhoid fever are reported annually, mostly in developing countries.

DIFFERENT TYPES OF *SALMONELLA*

When Jim met with his doctor, the doctor explained that it was *Salmonella* that caused Jim's disease symptoms. *Salmonella* are rod-shaped bacteria that are related to the common intestinal bacterium, *Escherichia coli*. *Salmonella* are characterized as gram-negative and flagellated (Figure 5.1). The most current classification suggests only a single species of *Salmonella* (*Salmonella enterica*). Although only a single species of *Salmonella* exists, there are many "serovars." A serovar is a specific set of O and H antigens. Human diseases caused by *Salmonella* fall into two categories—the enteric fever group and the **gastroenteritis** group.

Enteric fever organisms cause a number of symptoms affecting many parts of the body. Such diseases are called systemic illnesses. Fever and headache are common. Diarrhea is usually not present. Bacteria are commonly found in the bloodstream. The enteric fever serovars are not found in animals but are easily spread by contaminated water. The number of organisms needed to cause the symptoms, known as the infectious dose, is small. Unfortunately, enteric fever *Salmonella* may continue to be shed in fecal matter for months or

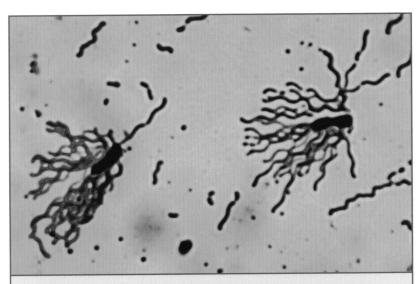

Figure 5.1 *Salmonella typhi* is a gram-negative, rod-shaped organism. Because it is gram-negative and will not retain the initial purple stain (see discussion in Chapter 2), the bacteria appear pinkish red.

years from chronic carriers (recall from Chapter 1 the story of Typhoid Mary).

Typhoid fever and paratyphoid fever are known as enteric fevers. Serological tests are used for diagnosis and antibiotics are needed to treat the disease effectively. Vaccines effectively prevent typhoid fever.

By contrast, gastroenteritis serovars are found in the gastrointestinal tract of animals and require a large, infectious dose. *Salmonella enterica* var Typhimurium (formerly known as *Salmonella typhimirium*) and *Salmonella enterica* var Enteritidis (formerly known as *Salmonella enteritidis*) are the most common gastroenteritis serovars. Since the organisms are killed by heat, they are not normally found in properly cooked food. Antibiotics are usually not required, and rehydration is usually an effective treatment. There are no serological tests for diagnosis or good vaccines against the gastroenteritis *Salmonellas*.

Jim quickly recognized that his symptoms and test results indicated enteric fever *Salmonella*. Thankfully, antibiotics effectively treat the disease. The strain of organism that infected Jim resembled two strains that were rampant in Calcutta and Bombay in 1990–1991. As people moved from those cities to New Delhi looking for better living and working conditions, carriers introduced the bacteria to the New Delhi area.

THE DISCOVERY AND USE OF ANTIBIOTICS

The first antibiotic that was safely used on humans was discovered in 1928 by Alexander Fleming. It came from a common airborne mold and became known as penicillin. Woodward and colleagues described the first successful treatment of typhoid fever using a chemical extracted from a mold in 1948. This mold and the chemicals produced by it, referred to as antibiotics, were discovered by scientists Paul Burkholder and Dick Benedict. Over the years more of these antibiotics were discovered. Most came from molds, including the one that would work against the typhoid organism. Antibiotics work by killing bacteria directly (**bactericidal**) or by inhibiting the growth and reproduction of bacteria (**bacteriostatic**). Chloromycetin was soon synthesized and renamed chloramphenicol. Chloramphenicol tends to inhibit the growth and reproduction of bacteria rather than killing them directly. Chloramphenicol inhibits production of bacterial proteins.

Chloramphenicol may cause two different types of bone marrow depression, resulting in anemia (reduced red blood cell count). One form is dose-related and interferes with iron metabolism. Since iron is essential to production of red blood cells, interference with iron metabolism has a negative effect on red blood cell production. This form occurs most frequently in patients taking high doses for protracted periods of time. Patients with liver disease are also likely to exhibit this type of anemia. Fortunately this form is reversible. An irreversible form of **aplastic anemia** occurs in about 1 out of every 25,000 patients.

Chloramphenicol is effective against both gram-positive and gram-negative bacteria. Antibiotics that work against both gram-positive and gram-negative organisms are said to be broad-spectrum in their action. Chloramphenicol produces fairly rapid

ANTIBIOTICS EFFECTIVE AGAINST TYPHOID BACTERIA

Using chloramphenicol against the typhoid bacteria does not diminish the chance of a person becoming a carrier, even though it may cure the person of having an active form of the disease. Ampicillin, amoxicillin, and co-trimoxazole, on the other hand, reduce the risk of the carrier condition and have very few side effects. Ampicillin and amoxicillin are known as semi-synthetic penicillins. They share the basic chemical backbone found in the penicillin molecule and have had chemical groups added to that backbone. These added side groups are synthesized chemically. Since they are so similar to penicillin, patients who are allergic to penicillin should not use any of the semi-synthetic penicillins. All the semi-synthetic penicillins have been shown as effective as chloramphenicol in curing patients.

The antibiotics mentioned have the added benefit of being relatively inexpensive. As mentioned earlier in the chapter, the major drawback to the use of any of these three antibiotics is the increased resistance to their action by bacteria.

Jim's strain was resistant to chloramphenicol, ampicillin and amoxicillin, tetracycline, and trimethoprim-sulphamethoxazole, also known as co-trimoxazole. At least one analysis of typhoid cases in the United States showed that 25% of the cases were resistant to one or more antibiotics. The same study concluded that ciprofloxacin and ceftriaxone are the most appropriate drugs to treat typhoid fever.

Marta-Louise Ackers, et al. "Laboratory-Based Surveillance of Salmonella Serotype Typhi Infections in the United States: Antimicrobial Resistance on the Rise." *Journal of the American Medical Association*, 283:20. (May 24, 2000): 2668–2673.

improvement in a patient's general condition and cures about 90% of patients. Bacteria are cleared from the bloodstream within a few hours and from the stool in a few days.

Jim's doctor gave Jim a prescription for a low dose of ciprofloxacin (Cipro®), which is the drug of choice for cases of multi-drug resistant microbes. This antibiotic is not recommended for young children. Another antibiotic called ceftriaxone is considered the best choice for young children.

Ciprofloxacin belongs to a group of antibiotics known as quinolones, which effectively kill a broad range of organisms. They work by inhibiting the production of enzymes needed to repair and reproduce the bacterial DNA. While taking ciprofloxacin, Jim would have to monitor what he ate or drank to avoid potential interactions. He loved coffee, but it looked like he would need to stay away from caffeine products during his 10-day course of ciprofloxacin because caffeine could cause undesirable or dangerous results. Ciprofloxacin seems to decrease the elimination of caffeine from the body, causing an increase in caffeine in the blood stream. Irritability and sleeplessness are two of the possible problems related to the higher blood caffeine level. Jim would have to read beverage and food labels carefully to limit his ingestion of caffeine. Perhaps he would just drink lots of water.

Jim would also have to take some of his mineral supplements at least two hours before he took the ciprofloxacin. Calcium, copper, iron, manganese, and zinc bind up the antibiotic, decreasing the absorption of the antibiotic into the bloodstream. He would also have to avoid various antacids like Maalox®, Mylanta®, Tums®, and Rolaids®, which have been shown to bind with a number of antibiotics, reducing their effectiveness.

Jim was being given ciprofloxacin because of its effectiveness and his age. If he had been under twelve years of age, he would have been given another antibiotic because ciprofloxacin and other quinolones can cause cartilage damage in growing animals.

The antibiotic Jim would have been given if he were younger is called ceftriaxone, known commercially as Rocephin®. It belongs to a family of antibiotics called the cephalosporins. Cephalosporins prevent bacterial cell wall formation, which causes the internal osmotic pressures inside the cell to increase so the cell bursts open. Ceftriaxone does not show any cartilage-related problems for children. Ceftriaxone has shown excellent killing power both in laboratory tests and in human subjects. One study even showed that taking ceftriaxone for five days was as effective as taking chloramphenicol for fourteen days.

The United States Food and Drug Administration (FDA) is just one organization that provides general information about resistance of microorganisms to antibiotics. Resistance is due largely to the increased overuse, misuse, and abuse of antibiotics, and will be discussed in detail in Chapter 7. **Antibiotic resistance** (Figure 5.2) is of great concern to the medical community because more and more bacteria are becoming increasingly resistant to specific antibiotics. The implications include not having an antibiotic that is effective against a disease-causing bacterium or having to use a combination of antibiotics to kill the bacteria. Keep in mind that antibiotics are identified as foreign molecules by our immune system. Over time, the immune system may begin to develop antibodies against the antibiotics with the possibility of a severe and potentially deadly reaction. Scientists are researching strategies for combating antibiotic resistance.

The Centers for Disease Control and Prevention (CDC) and the University of Wisconsin also provide helpful fact sheets and overviews online. The CDC Website contains several papers outlining general recommendations about how the problem can be contained with the cooperation of doctors, hospitals, and increased public awareness.

As a health systems administration major, Jim was

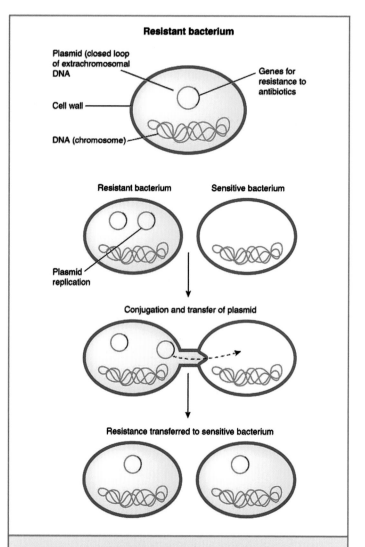

Figure 5.2 Bacterial cells containing plasmids with information about resistance to specific antibiotics may transfer copies of that information to other bacteria. One method of transfer is illustrated here. A copy of the genetic information in the plasmid is copied (replicated), and the copy is sent by means of a specific protein tube called a sex pilus or conjugation tube. After transfer, the tube is removed, and the second bacterium now has a copy of information about how to become resistant to specific antibiotics.

particularly interested in the CDC online article entitled "Addressing the Antibiotic Resistance Problem."[1] A number of recommendations were put forth that Jim knew he would be dealing with when he entered the workforce. The National Institutes of Health (NIH) had a fact sheet entitled "Antibiotic Resistance Fact Sheet" that was also interesting.[2] However, the article that caused a cold sweat to break out on Jim's body was entitled "Miracle Drugs vs. Superbugs."[3] The FDA provided an extensive listing of microbes in a number of categories that had become resistant to many current antibiotics. In many cases, medical science already had or was close to reaching the point where current antibiotics were unable to keep up with new resistant forms of bacteria. As Jim read on, he realized the importance of educating the public about the proper use of antibiotics.

Jim knew he had been fortunate to receive prompt medical treatment from a well-informed doctor. He would recover from his bout with typhoid fever without any long-term negative effects. But he was also concerned that millions of people in the world did not have access to this type of care or did not have adequate health insurance to pay for it.

6

Preventing Typhoid Fever

Jim tried to figure out what he could have done differently to avoid contracting typhoid fever. For most diseases, vaccination (if available) is usually the best avenue to follow to avoid contracting a disease. However, no vaccine can or should act as a substitute for common sense, good background information about the area, and careful selection of what you eat or drink when you are in an area that may be contaminated.

Typhoid vaccination (Figure 6.1) is not required but is recommended if traveling into areas where typhoid fever is endemic. Jim did not get vaccinated because he thought he would be in New Delhi or other large cities where typhoid fever had not been a problem. He did not anticipate going into rural and urban slum areas. Despite Jim's careful preparation for his trip to India, this oversight caused him considerable discomfort.

TYPES OF VACCINES AVAILABLE

Vaccination against typhoid fever is not 100% effective. Two typhoid vaccines are currently available in the United States. The first is an oral vaccine that uses live but weakened (attenuated), bacteria. It is known as the Vivotif Berna® vaccine. The unusual name refers to the company and its location, Berna Biotech in Bern, Switzerland. The vivotif portion refers to live (vivo) typhoid bacteria (tif). There have been attempts in recent years to use other strains for vaccines, with good success. Avant Immunotherapeutics received permission from the National Institutes of Health (NIH) in January 2003 to continue **pre-clinical** development of Ty800, a single-dose, oral typhoid vaccine.

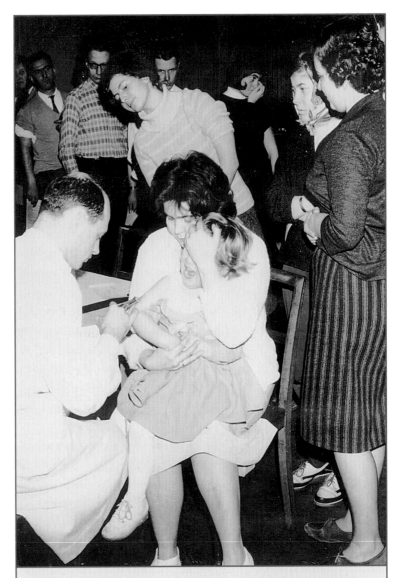

Figure 6.1 Before traveling to areas where typhoid fever is present, it is best to be vaccinated against the disease. Because the disease is very rare in the United States, the typhoid vaccine is not included in the routine vaccination schedule. This little girl from Germany is getting the typhoid vaccination, possibly because she will be traveling to a more rural country.

The Swiss Serum and Vaccine Institute produces the current vaccine. This vaccine consists of a total of four capsules, which should be taken one every other day and must be taken in a very specific manner. All four doses must be taken to insure maximum protection. Each capsule must be swallowed about one hour before a meal but not chewed. The capsule protects the vaccine against stomach acid so the vaccine remains in an active state when it reaches the intestine. The capsules must be kept cool, between 35–46°F, or the vaccine becomes inactivated. Thus they should be taken with cool to cold water, not hot tea or coffee.

Side effects of this vaccine include abdominal distress, nausea, vomiting, and hives or rash. The vaccine is not given if the person has a fever, nausea, vomiting, or diarrhea. People currently taking or about to start taking antibiotics or anti-malarial drugs should not get the vaccine. Pregnant or nursing mothers and immunocompromised patients, such as those with **HIV** or **AIDS**, also should not take the vaccine. Research suggests protection rates of between 50 and 80%. Protection should last about five years. In the United States, this vaccine is not approved for children less than six years of age.

The second vaccine, sometimes called a **subunit vaccine**, is made from polysaccharide material in the capsule of the microbe. It is called Typhim Vi™ and is manufactured by the pharmaceutical company Aventis Pasteur. It is also known as the Vi capsular polysaccharide antigen (ViCPS) vaccine. The vaccine became available in February 1995 and is given with a single shot into the muscle of the arm. Minimal side effects include redness and swelling at the site of the injection and the possibility of a slight fever and headache. People who have a fever or who have had a severe reaction to a previous dose of this vaccine should not be given the vaccine. The vaccine is not recommended for children under two years of age. The protection rate for this vaccine is also in the range of 50 to 80% and lasts about two years.

A new combination vaccine on the market since October 2001 combines Typhim Vi™ for typhoid fever and Avaxim™ for hepatitis A. Protection starts within 14 days of the injection. Another important milestone in the fight against typhoid fever also occurred in 2001. The April 26, 2001, issue of the *New England Journal of Medicine* included an article entitled "The Efficacy of a *Salmonella typhi* Vi Conjugate Vaccine in Two-to-Five-Year-Old Children." The report outlined the effectiveness of a new vaccine for children younger than six years of age. It had the highest reported effectiveness (91.5%) of any existing typhoid vaccine. Dr. Duane Alexander, director of NIH's National Institute of Child Health and Development (NICHD) felt so strongly about this vaccine that he suggested that: "We have achieved a two-fold victory in the world public health. Not only is this the first vaccine to protect young children against typhoid fever, it appears to be the most effective typhoid vaccine ever developed. In contrast to other typhoid vaccines, it is virtually free of side effects." More than 11,000 Vietnamese children, ages 2 to 5, were part of the study. This area of the world was chosen because there are always many cases of typhoid fever in the area each year. Children younger than two were to be tested during 2002 with results due sometime in 2004.[4]

RISKY BUSINESS

Jim knew that being vaccinated was only half the battle against typhoid fever. Being informed and having common sense were also important. Jim knew by now that watching what he ate or drank when he traveled was just as important in preventing exposure to disease-causing bacteria, perhaps even more so, than getting vaccinated.

Jim could probably have avoided contracting typhoid fever if he had not eaten certain foods while he was in India. However, one of the most prevalent travelers' diseases, malaria, is not transmitted in food or water, but by mosquitoes. Jim had been prepared for mosquitoes, plastering himself with mosquito repellant every day. He had been careful about drinking water or melting ice to avoid cholera, dysentery, hepatitis A, and traveler's diarrhea. But he made a painful mistake when he ate a sandwich that

VACCINE DEVELOPMENT

Many bacteria have an outer coating or capsule that contains polysaccharides. The capsules make it difficult for white blood cells to engulf or phagocytize the bacteria and destroy them. The immune system of young children normally does not recognize polysaccharides easily. It is not clear why the immune system cells of young children do not respond to the capsule. Researchers found that by linking a foreign protein to the polysaccharides, the immune system is activated to produce antibodies against the proteins and the polysaccharides. These antibodies will attach to the surface of the capsule and help the white blood cells destroy the bacteria.

The conjugate Vi typhoid vaccine was developed using the same technique used to create the Hib vaccine. The Hib vaccine provides protection against *Haemophilus influenzae* type B, a bacterium that is a leading cause of meningitis in South and Central Asian countries like Vietnam. The polysaccharide covering *Haemophilus influenzae* type B is called the Vi polysaccharide, or Vi antigen. Previous studies showed that making antibodies against the Vi antigen would provide long-term immunity to the typhoid bacteria.

was offered in friendship but that exposed Jim to the typhoid bacteria.

Typhoid bacteria are commonly found in water, ice, food milk, and soil, where they may survive from two to seven days. In ice and ice cream, the bacteria can survive a month; in soil fertilized with sewage, typhoid bacteria can survive for more than two months. Typhoid bacteria can grow in milk without altering its taste or consistency and can live on the surface of vegetables washed in contaminated water for more than a day. One of the phrases that Jim had read several times was "Boil it, cook it, peel it, or forget it." Too bad he had not followed this advice that day while working in the urban slum area of New Delhi (Figure 6.2).

Jim found it hard to believe, but even ice cream was responsible for an outbreak of typhoid fever. In August 2002, typhoid bacteria afflicted 150 people in the Batken region of Kirghizia. All of the victims were celebrating the republic's Independence Day from the former Soviet Union. They all had eaten ice cream that had been carelessly prepared and was of poor quality.

Jim realized that he had not paid close attention to many of the warnings that he had read before going to India. His former biology professor had once told him that he needed to consider good and useful information as he would consider a gourmet meal. Do not eat it when you are upset because you will miss the subtle flavors. Do not eat it when you are excited because you will forget what it tasted like. Do not eat it quickly or you will not appreciate what you had. Take it in small bites and savor the flavor and essence of the total meal. At the time Jim did not understand what a good meal had to do with understanding and retaining information. He was beginning to understand now. He had seen the same information over and over and never read it very carefully or completely.

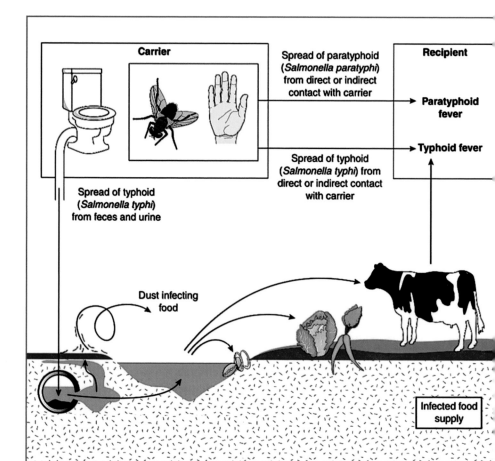

Figure 6.2 The process of typhoid transmission is illustrated here. Typhoid carriers spread organisms through their feces. Flies may land on the feces and spread the organisms, or humans may transmit the organisms through fecal matter that is transferred on unwashed hands. Poor wastewater treatment may cause water supplies to become contaminated. Raw vegetables grown on sewage irrigated fields may also lead to infection of humans and other animals. This can also lead to infected cows and possibly infected milk from those cows.

The irony was that several sources said pretty much the same thing.

- Water—if you drink water, buy it bottled or canned. Carbonated water is safer than non-carbonated (probably due to the carbonic acid formed when carbon dioxide dissolves in water). Boil water for three minutes or have tea or coffee made with boiled water. Ask for drinks without ice, unless the ice is made from bottled or boiled water. Avoid frozen juice bars and flavored ices that may have been made with contaminated water.

- Food—Eat food that has been thoroughly cooked (at least 165°F in the center of any food to destroy protein toxins produced by bacteria), preferably while it is still hot and steaming. Avoid raw vegetables and fruits that cannot be peeled. If you peel them yourself, wash your hands with soap before and after you do the peeling. Do not eat the peelings. Avoid lettuce and leafy vegetables that are easily contaminated and difficult to wash well.

- Vendors—Avoid food and beverages from street vendors. It is difficult to keep food clean on the street. In Jim's case, the obvious extension of this rule is to not take or eat food from well-meaning family members living in slum areas.

- Environment—Keep the surroundings clean and clear of trash and feces to avoid creating breeding areas for flies and mosquitoes.

Adapted from the CDC's Typhoid Fever
Disease Information page, located at
www.cdc.gov/ncidod/dbmd/diseaseinfo/typhoidfever_g.htm

Jim remembered the tremendous number of flies in and around the slum areas. Flies help spread the typhoid bacteria because they land in fecal matter and transfer germs to whatever surface, including food, they land on next.

IMPEDIMENTS TO PREVENTION
Jim thought back to his time in India and realized that a number of problems in South and Central Asia and in other developing countries made it difficult to prevent the spread of food- and waterborne diseases. For example, poor farmers in some of these areas use human sewage as fertilizer. In addition, inadequate sewage systems allow human and animal wastes to overflow into water wells. Rivers are often used for many different and incompatible purposes, such as washing clothes, sewage disposal, and drinking. Sewage often contaminates the water used to irrigate rice paddies and runs off into coastal waters to contaminate shellfish in the area.

THE ORIGINAL SWAT TEAM

The housefly was shown to be a carrier of typhoid bacteria in the late nineteenth century. The State Health Commissioner of Utah at that time, Dr. Theodore B. Beatty, began a campaign to eradicate the housefly. After giving talks and passing out literature, he started a contest to see who could kill the most flies. The winner of the contest won $1,000 donated by a businessman from Salt Lake City. The winner brought in 707 quarts of dead flies, which represented an estimated 9.5 million flies. In all, the citizens of Utah brought in 3,715 quarts of flies. In spite of reducing the fly population temporarily, real progress finally was made when breeding sites, such as primitive toilet facilities, were destroyed.

Miriam B. Murphy. "Salt Lake City Had its Typhoid Mary." *History Blazer.* April 1996. Accessed at *http://historytogo.utah.gov*

What are the problems currently associated with the transmission and treatment of typhoid fever? What are some of the new initiatives, both local and global, that may positively impact and change the course of this disease? What are some of the new treatments and therapies that are being developed? These and other topics will be discussed in the final chapters in the book as we look at concerns and hopes for the future.

7

The Problems of Antibiotic Resistance

As mentioned in Chapter 5, antibiotics are chemicals that are produced by living organisms, usually fungi or bacteria, which destroy or inhibit other microorganisms or their ability to reproduce. One of the most distressing developments that have occurred since the mid-1950s is the increasing numbers of microbes that have become resistant to an increasing number of antibiotics. The initial relief that came from conquering disease using antibiotics such as penicillin and streptomycin became muted as more microbes found ways to neutralize or inactivate the antibiotics.

Microorganisms have lived in proximity to each other in the soil and water for millions of years. Often they compete for the same scarce resources. To succeed in such a competitive environment, microorganisms found biochemical means of destroying or inactivating chemicals produced by other organisms. This ongoing process in which one organism produces destructive chemicals and another finds ways to destroy it is nature's way of maintaining a balance among the microbes in the soil and water.

The two main issues to address regarding resistance are why and how resistance occurs.

WHY RESISTANCE OCCURS

Simply put, antibiotic resistance develops due to the abuse, misuse, and overuse of antibiotics. Antibiotics are ineffective against viruses, yet patients often pester their doctors to prescribe antibiotics for viral maladies, including colds or influenza. If antibiotics are taken for a viral infection, they destroy some of the helpful bacteria in the intestines. Bacteria, both "good" and "bad," are in a constant competition within the intestines. Destruction of the "good guys" provides opportunity for the unfettered growth of the "bad guys."

Another problem with the use of antibiotics occurs when the patient fails to follow instructions. When antibiotics are prescribed, the patient is instructed to take all of the antibiotics provided. Often patients stop taking antibiotics as soon as they start feeling better, even though there are still more antibiotics to be taken. By not completing a course of antibiotics, only the least resistant of the offending bacteria are killed off, leaving the most resistant. The more resistant bacteria survive and reproduce so that next time it will take a higher dosage or different antibiotic to kill the same bacteria.

A third reason why microorganisms become resistant to antibiotics is when antibiotics are used in low doses in livestock and agriculture. Often antibiotics are mixed with animal feed. The amounts are too small to be used for treating a disease, but they do destroy the least hardy bacteria. The most resistant bacteria survive. Part of the rationale for giving livestock antibiotics is to keep them healthy and allow them to grow rapidly without competition from internal parasites in the form of intestinal bacteria. This leads to increased profits for the company that owns the livestock. Antibiotic residues are often found on fruits and vegetables that have been sprayed to reduce premature decomposition. If we are not careful about washing fruits and vegetables before we eat them, we may kill off some of our useful bacteria, allowing the more resistant and harmful organisms to survive. On June 3, 2002, the *New York Times* ran a story entitled "Monitoring Antibiotic in Shrimp." The story commented on the discovery of chloramphenicol in shrimp imported from Asia. Agricultural use of this antibiotic is banned in the United States, because it has been shown to cause such problems as childhood leukemia. So far, officials say that only a small percentage of the imported shrimp have been found to contain trace amounts of this antibiotic. However, its presence in food is a serious concern. The problem is that chloramphenicol in any amount is being found and transported to other countries that may have less stringent detection and enforcement policies for imported foods.

Finally, antibiotics may be available without a prescription in some countries. If a person taking an antibiotic is not aware of the limitations and potential problems associated with the antibiotic, he or she may be creating an environment in which resistant organisms not only survive a course of antibiotics, but actually grow more resistant over time.

HOW RESISTANCE DEVELOPS

Microorganisms have a marvelous ability to adapt to new and changing environmental conditions very rapidly. They often have a reproductive rate that doubles their numbers in minutes. Both *Escherichia coli* and *Staphylococcus aureus* can double their numbers every 12–20 minutes when optimum conditions exist.

Bacteria have an extremely flexible genetic program. It consists of a single chromosome and a number of small chunks of DNA called **plasmids**, which look like miniature chromosomes. Plasmids contain a limited number of genes that are often genetic codes for enzymes and other proteins that provide resistance to one more antibiotics.

Bacteria can become resistant in several ways (Figure 7.1). One of the ways that bacteria develop resistance to antibiotics is through mutations of their genetic information or DNA. A single mutation can spread through a population of bacteria in a matter of hours. If that mutation provides a way for

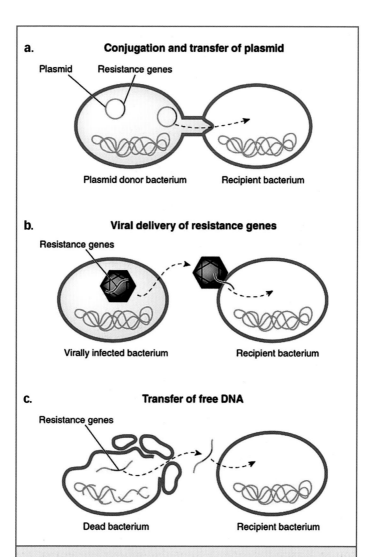

Figure 7.1 In the process of conjugation (a), copies of plasmids, like pages copied from a book, are transferred to another bacterium. The second bacterium now contains a copy of new genetic information. In the process of transduction (b), viruses infecting one bacterium construct new viruses containing some of the bacterial information and transmit it to new bacteria that they infect. During transformation (c), DNA from a dead bacterium is incorporated into the genetic program of a recipient bacterium.

bacteria to survive in the presence of a particular antibiotic, that genetic change will soon be found in millions of new resistant bacteria. When bacteria die, other bacteria often scavenge the DNA of the dead microbe and incorporate it into their own genetic programs. Called **transformation**, this new information may contain genetic codes for inactivating or neutralizing various antibiotics.

Some bacteria can exchange copies of plasmids. A copy of a plasmid is passed through a protein tube called a pilus into another bacterium (the process of conjugation), making it possible to exchange genetic information between live bacteria (Figure 7.2). In a sense, this is the first information highway; it has been active for millions, perhaps billions, of years. Some of this new genetic information may provide the recipient bacterium with a competitive advantage in its environment.

Bacteria often are infected by specific viruses. As a virus infects one bacterium, it takes over the cell and forces the bacterium to produce and assemble new virus parts. As the new virus is constructed, it may incorporate some of the bacterial DNA into its own genetic program. The next time the new viruses infect other bacteria, they may leave some of the incorporated bacterial DNA in the newly infected bacterium. This process is called **transduction** and, like the others mentioned earlier, this method provides new genetic information to a bacterium that may allow it to become resistant to one or more antibiotics.

Bacteria have evolved a number of mechanisms at the molecular level that allow them to resist antibiotics.

- Often an antibiotic must attach to a particular structure such as the cell wall or a protein receptor in the cell membrane. If the bacterium changes the target molecule in some way, the antibiotic will not be able to attach to the bacterium and will be ineffective.

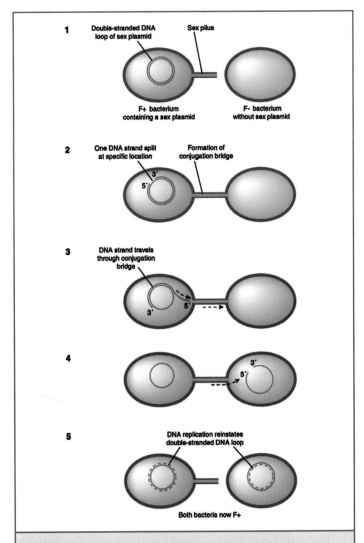

Figure 7.2 Plasmids are transferred horizontally from an infected host (+) to an uninfected recipient (-). The sex pilus serves as a protein tube bridge between the cells. One strand of the double-stranded DNA in the + cell opens up and crosses the bridge. Once the DNA strand is in the previously uninfected cell, the cells separate and the DNA in each cell replicates a complementary strand, leaving each cell with an identical copy of double-stranded DNA.

- Some bacteria take the antibiotic into their cells and surround it with a membrane of proteins. This effectively prevents the antibiotic from interfering with a biochemical process or locking on to a receptor molecule.

- Certain bacteria produce chemicals—e.g., enzymes—that inactivate or destroy the drug. One example is gonorrhea microbes that produce a chemical called penicillinase, which neutralizes penicillin. These microbes are designated as PPNG, penicillinase producing *Neisseria gonorrhea.*

- Other species of bacteria may contain structures—e.g., a capsule—that keep the antibiotic from penetrating into the cell.

- Some bacteria have molecular pumps that actively remove antibiotics or other unwanted chemicals from the cell.

CURRENT RESEARCH

The National Institute of Allergy and Infectious Diseases (NIAID) is a component of the National Institutes of Health (NIH). A major part of its job is to support research efforts to prevent, diagnose, and treat infectious and immune-mediated illnesses. NIAID supports research to study the molecular mechanisms responsible for drug resistance and to develop new chemical interventions for disease treatment and prevention. Since 1992, its research funding for anti-microbial resistance research has nearly doubled to nearly $14 million.

Research using gene-sequencing techniques can identify the critical molecules involved in microbial reproduction. These molecules may then serve as targets for new drugs. Research conducted so far in the area of drug resistance has led to a variety of important discoveries:

- Discovery of methods that will make it possible to reverse resistance to antibiotics.

- Understanding of the genetic reasons why some parasites become resistant and the ability to recognize the organisms that are, in fact, resistant.

- New molecular level mechanisms and tools make it easier to recognize those species that are resistant to specific drugs.

- The creation of new drugs to combat the drug-resistant strains of *Plasmodium*, the organism responsible for the disease malaria.

Adapted from: "Antimicrobial Resistance."
Bethesda, Md.: Office of Communications and Public
Liaison, National Institute of Allergy and Infectious
Diseases, National Institutes of Health, Accessed at:
www.niaid.nih.gov/factsheets/antimicro.htm.

NIAID recently cosponsored a meeting with the National Aeronautics and Space Administration (NASA), the Defense Advanced Research Projects Agency, and the University of Alabama on emerging infections and anti-microbial resistance. The meeting was designed to stimulate research in drug design and discuss strategies for developing new drugs against bacteria, fungi, viruses, and other parasites.

CDC research has shown that the incidence of typhoid fever in United States citizens traveling to the Indian subcontinent was about 18 times higher than in any other geographic region. From 1985 to 1994, the number of cultures of *Salmonella typhi* that were resistant to the three major antibiotics (chloramphenicol, ampicillin, and trimethoprim-sulfamethoxazole) more than doubled. A few years later, a report in the *Journal of the American Medical Association*, May 2000, showed that 25% of all cases were resistant to one or more antibiotics and 17% were resistant to five or more antibiotics.

The CDC also reported in December 2000 that typhoid bacteria resistant to the five major antibiotics used against the disease emerged between 1997 and 1999 in Kenya. Because these antibiotics are routinely used to fight other diseases, it will be necessary to begin using fluoroquinolones against the typhoid bacteria.

Between 1990 and 1991 in Calcutta, India, 92% of the cultured typhoid strains showed multi-drug resistance. Calcutta and its suburbs continue to be endemic for the disease. Endemic refers to the fact that the disease is constantly present in the population in low numbers. In April 2001, the National Institute of Child Health and Human Development (NICHD), part of the NIH, reported that typhoid fever continues to be "a lingering public health threat in the United States." (Figure 7.3) The evidence is clear that resistant forms of *Salmonella typhi* represent a real danger in developing countries of the world. By extension, multi-drug resistant typhoid bacteria continue to be a problem in the United States because so many people travel between continents.

WHAT CAN WE DO?

Bacteria hitch a ride on fecal matter, which in turn contaminates food and water and spreads diseases such as typhoid fever. To prevent fecal matter from getting into food or water, it is necessary to improve basic sanitation and hygiene. The World Health Organization (WHO), in its "Fact Sheet N149" from March 1997, set forth some common sense guidelines for preventing the spread of disease-causing bacteria.[5]

- Public water supplies need to be protected from contamination, both physically and legislatively.

- Chemical treatment of the water supply is usually necessary, and chlorine is the chemical of choice.

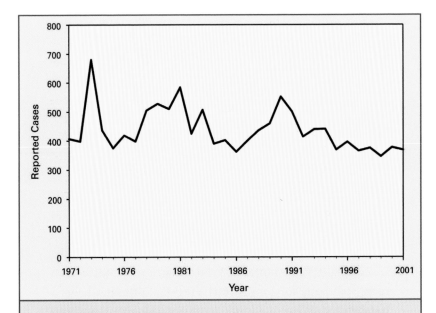

Figure 7.3 Although the number of typhoid cases in recent years is not as high as it once was (as in the early 1970s), it still continues to exist in the United States. Many of these outbreaks may be from travelers returning from countries where typhoid fever is more common. This chart shows the number of reported typhoid cases in the United States from 1971–2001.

- Provide safe water supplies and avoid possible back flow connections between sewers and water supplies.

- Fecal waste from humans and animals should be removed carefully and with the use of proper sanitary procedures. Latrines should be properly covered and chemically treated to avoid the entrance and growth of flies, which may subsequently spread disease organisms from the feces.

- Be sure that the area and utensils you use for food preparation are clean before you use them and wash them frequently while they are being used. Don't forget your hands also.

• Perhaps more than any other single health measure, the simple act of washing one's hands after going to the bathroom is among the most important in combating the spread of disease-causing bacteria. Anyone involved in working with food and the public in general needs to be constantly reminded of how important this act is in terms of preventing the spread of the disease organism.

A public drinking water supply is defined as a system that provides piped water for human consumption to at least 25 individuals. In the United States, public water supplies are checked for about 90 contaminants, as specified in the Federal Safe Drinking Water Act and administered by the United States Environmental Protection Agency. Water must meet standards for human consumption although it need not be pure. Water is disinfected using chlorine, usually in

WILL TYPHOID FEVER BE NEXT?

In May 2002, a *New York Times* headline read "New Resistant Gonorrhea Migrating to Mainland U.S." The article detailed the move of resistant bacteria from Asia to Hawaii to California. The natural host for gonorrhea, like typhoid fever, is humans. Between 60 and 80% of the gonorrhea organisms from East Asian countries were resistant to fluoroquinolones such as Cipro. The most effective treatment for gonorrhea had been Cipro. However, since fluoroquinolones can no longer be used against the gonorrhea organisms, the cephalosporins will have to bear the major treatment burden. If only one chemical treatment is effective against a group of bacteria, it is only a matter of time before those bacteria become resistant to that treatment.

David Kirby. "New Resistant Gonorrhea Migrating to Mainland U.S." *New York Times*, Late Edition—Final , Section F , Page 5 , Column 1. May 7, 2002.

the form of chloramines (a combination of chlorine and ammonia). Many cities such as Philadelphia saw a dramatic decline in the cases of typhoid fever when they began disinfection procedures after 1905.

Chlorination effectively kills most pathogens such as *Salmonella typhi* and helps control the growth of such organisms within the pipes of the distribution system. As we will see in the next chapter, keeping bacteria such as *Salmonella typhi* out of the food supply is not as easy as disinfecting water.

8

Future Concerns

Since September 11, 2001, the world has become even more concerned about the use of biological and chemical agents that can cause mass destruction. This concern, while heightened since the terrorist attacks on the United States, is not new. In 1972, members of an extremist group known as "The Order of the Rising Sun" were arrested and found to possess cultures of *Salmonella typhi*. They had planned to contaminate the water supplies of major mid-western cities, including Chicago and St. Louis.[6] In 1939, the Japanese biological warfare unit known as Unit 731 added *Salmonella typhi* to rivers on the border between Manchuria and the Soviet Union. The terror caused by any disease organism that can inflict major damage and sometimes death is no less a concern if it is caused by planned terrorist attacks or unintended actions of unknowing individuals.

COMBATING DISEASE AT ITS SOURCE

Research by Kidgell et al. shows that *Salmonella typhi* is approximately 50,000 years old. It appears to have developed during the hunter-gatherer stage of human development, before agriculture was organized or animals were domesticated. Humans continue to be its only known animal host.

Typhoid fever is a disease that transcends race, gender, age, ethnicity, or religious preference. It is an equal opportunity infection. But some people are much more likely to become afflicted as the result of their economic or geographic circumstances. As the nineteenth century came to a close, public health practitioners were of two minds as to the cause of disease. One group believed that dirt and filth was the cause, while the other thought that microorganisms caused disease.

Even though they disagreed about disease causes, these two groups together brought about important changes that effectively reduced the incidence and impact of diseases in the twentieth century. The first group encouraged the development of massive sanitation projects in cities. Sewage disposal, garbage collection, vaccination programs, and sanitation practices at hospitals, clinics, and dispensaries became a part of the solution. The second group was concerned with disease transmission, so they implemented policies that led to medical inspections, laboratory testing of milk, and quarantine of infected patients.

Several individuals in the mid-1800s, including William Budd, demonstrated that typhoid fever was caused by bacteria that infect food or water. In those cities that instituted sanitation projects and water filtration systems, the occurrence of typhoid fever decreased. As a result, typhoid fever is rarely found in developed or industrialized countries today. Better sanitation, better personal hygiene, better medical care and testing, and water treatment in developed countries all have reduced the presence of the bacteria that cause the disease. Approximately 70 to 80% of all typhoid fever cases in the United States are imported from other countries.

Worldwide, between 10 and 17 million cases of typhoid fever are reported annually, resulting in about 600,000 deaths. In developing countries, typhoid fever is constantly present (endemic), and is a continual public health menace. Since typhoid bacteria are spread by the fecal-oral route, inadequate personal hygiene and water contamination are major reasons why this disease is still a large health problem outside the United States. Better education about personal hygiene and proper disposal and treatment of waste, as well as water treatment and filtration, top the list of major reforms and actions that must be taken to eradicate typhoid fever from the worldwide population.

Of continuing concern to public health professionals are individuals who appear healthy but either had the disease and recovered from it, and individuals who have no memory of having the disease. This new generation of healthy carriers is now coming under scrutiny. In addition, a disturbing occurrence reported in April 2001 points to a new way to spread typhoid fever bacteria. The Centers for Disease Control and Prevention (CDC) documented a sexually transmitted outbreak of typhoid fever among gay men in Cincinnati, Ohio. A Cincinnati man had vacationed in Puerto Rico and contracted typhoid fever, which he then spread to seven other men with whom he had sexual contact. The CDC health officials believe the bacteria were spread through oral-anal contact since none of the men had shared food or drink.

TARGETS OF TYPHOID FEVER

In February 2002, more than 200 national and international delegates attended the Fifth International Symposium on Typhoid Fever and Other Salmonelloses, held at the Aga Khan University Hospital in Karachi, Pakistan, in collaboration with the World Health Organization (WHO). Talks focused on diagnosis, treatment, symptomology, and epidemiology. Dr. Gordon Dougan of the Imperial College in London, England, talked about the importance of improving public health facilities, and developing and making available better diagnostic tools, vaccines, and antibiotics. Dr. Dougan talked about the genetic studies that were under way to develop new vaccine strains and explore new diagnostic approaches. Many of the new testing and treatment techniques and chemicals are described in Chapter 9.

"Typhoid big problem in poor countries." *Dawn the Internet Edition.* February 7, 2002. Accessed at *http://www.dawn.com/2002/02/07/nat20.htm*

The World Health Organization (WHO) and public health researchers worldwide recognize that typhoid fever is a big problem in poor countries. Clean water, increased sanitation measures, and inclusion of typhoid fever in national vaccine programs are top priorities in the effort to eradicate typhoid fever worldwide.

Greater research efforts in affected countries and strong international collaboration are also needed to effectively combat typhoid fever. At the February 2002 International Symposium on Typhoid Fever and Other Salmonelloses, the WHO and other international funding agencies were encouraged to place greater emphasis on typhoid research, focusing on the increasing problem of drug resistance and the need for more effective vaccination strategies. Dr. Chris Parry of Oxford University indicated that the fluoroquinolones were still the drug of choice in fighting typhoid fever but resistance was becoming a problem.

Dr. Tikki Pang from the WHO, Geneva, Switzerland, spoke at the Symposium on Typhoid about a program called Diseases of the Most Impoverished (DOMI), which is coordinated by the International Vaccine Institute and funded by the Bill and Melinda Gates Foundation. The DOMI program was designed to accelerate the introduction of new vaccines into the developing countries of Asia, assure that the vaccine supply is adequate and safe, and develop internationally agreed-upon recommendations for vaccine use.

Typhoid fever is a particularly important public health problem in Pakistan and many of the developing countries of Asia, where it is a **pediatric** problem. Almost 70% of all cases occur among children. Dr. Zulfigar A. Bhutta, chairman of the Symposium Organizing Committee, stressed that nutrition plays a key role in fighting this disease. Grossly malnourished children were at greater risk of succumbing to disease complications.

EMERGING FOODBORNE DISEASES

Robert Tauxe of the Centers for Disease Control and Prevention in Atlanta, Georgia, described in a 2002 interview with PBS's *Frontline*, emerging foodborne diseases as an evolving public health challenge. His article entitled "Emerging Foodborne Diseases: An Evolving Public Health Challenge" looked at some of the major trends in the spread of foodborne disease and how we are trying to monitor and prevent them.[7] Simply educating the consumer about basic safety and hygiene is insufficient, because there is a long chain of events that brings food from the farms to the kitchen table. Along the way there are multiple opportunities for food to become contaminated.

In developed countries such as the United States, typhoid fever was controlled by disinfection of drinking water, sewage treatment, milk sanitation and pasteurization, and shellfish bed sanitation. But while typhoid fever was being controlled, non-typhoid strains of *Salmonella* began to increase (Figure 8.1).

Fresh produce presents a new means of contamination. The irrigation water used for production and harvest may be tainted with human manure because there may not be sanitary bathroom facilities in the field for workers who pick and bundle the produce. Untreated or contaminated water may then be used for washing, spraying, and maintaining the appearance of produce. (Many shippers have now resorted to using chlorinated water to prevent contamination). The ice in the ice trucks used for distribution and transport may also be contaminated. And since fresh produce is often grown a long way from where it is finally purchased and consumed, it must be handled by more people on the way to market, increasing the risk that it will be contaminated. Finally, the water used in the final handling, slicing, shredding, squeezing, or peeling is often contaminated from continual human contact.

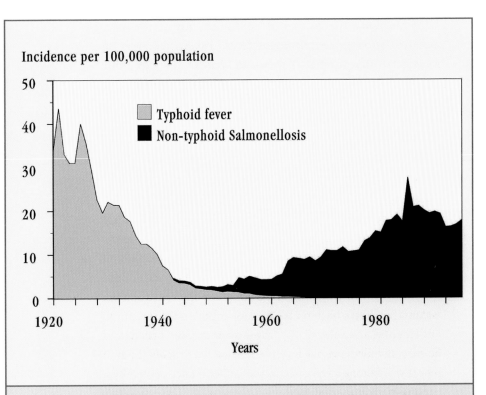

Incidence per 100,000 population

Figure 8.1 This graph shows the improvement in prevention of typhoid fever since 1920. This was the result of water and sewage treatment, milk pasteurization, and shellfish bed sanitation. Unfortunately, other foodborne infections have increased as typhoid has decreased. These include *Vibrio* bacteria in raw oysters, *Escherichia coli O157:H7* bacteria in hamburgers, and *Cyclospora* bacteria in Guatemalan raspberries.

Fortunately, some strategies are being applied to resolve these problems. The United States Department of Health and Human Services developed The Hazard Analysis and Critical Control Points (HACCP) strategy which attempts to identify and control the key points in the chain of events where contamination can either occur or be eliminated. This strategy is slowly replacing the final product inspection strategy.

Sometimes the source of contamination is not very obvious. During the winter of 1998–1999, there was an increase in the number of cases of typhoid fever in Dade County, Florida. This outbreak in the Miami area of Dade County was unusual because 16 people were infected in a very short period of time. There was no obvious connection between the victims other than that they were all Hispanic, as are 57% of the residents of that county. When the victims answered questionnaires, no common risk factors were found. But in conversations with the victims, it was found that they all had imbibed fruit shakes made from a tropical fruit called mamey. The shakes had been made with packaged fruit from manufacturing plants in Guatemala and Honduras. When tested, other packages of the product did not yield *Salmonella typhi* but did contain numerous coliform bacteria. Coliform bacteria are bacteria found in the intestines. Distribution and sales of the frozen mamey were halted, and no new cases of typhoid fever were reported. This is the first report of typhoid fever cases in the United States caused by a commercially imported food.[8]

WATERBORNE DISEASES

One concern that outweighs all others in this discussion of disease transmission is the prevalence of waterborne diseases. The March 2003 United Nations report of the World Water Forum in Kyoto, Japan, indicated that "The world's freshwater reserves are shrinking due to pollution, climate change and population growth." At that same World Water Forum in Kyoto, Japan, the United Nations reported that "In the next twenty years the average amount of water available for each person worldwide will drop by one-third." (Figure 8.2a)

More than two million people die each year due to diseases related to contaminated drinking water and poor sanitation. Increased pollution and warmer water temperatures due to global warming will worsen the problem as clean water becomes less available. The World Bank recently estimated that the equivalent of $600 billion is required to repair and improve the world's water delivery systems. However, sanitation has improved over the last 20 years, and this has led to a decrease in the prevalence of some diseases (Figure 8.2b)

According to Peter Gleick, president of the Pacific Institute for Studies in Development, Environment, and Security in Oakland, California, "The lack of access to safe drinking water and sanitation is directly related to poverty, and in many cases to the inability of governments to finance satisfactory water and sanitation systems." The direct and indirect human costs are many and include widespread health problems. Chapter 9 presents examples of new ideas, materials, and techniques that provide hope for the future. While the global water supply and the rural sector water supply have both increased, there are still more than 1 billion people in Africa, Asia, Latin America, and the Caribbean that have no access to improved water supplies. To meet proposed standards for 2015, water supplies will have to reach an additional 1.5 billion people, an increase of about 6%. In spite of an increase in the number of people with access to sanitation disposal, the number of people who lack access remains about the same. Rural sanitation coverage is less than one half that in the urban areas. By the year 2000, nearly 1.2 billion people lacked access to clean water, and nearly 2.4 billion lacked access to adequate santitation services. To achieve 2015 standards, more than 2.2 billion people will need to be provided with sanitation facilities in Africa, Asia, Latin America, and the Caribbean (refer again to Figure 8.2).

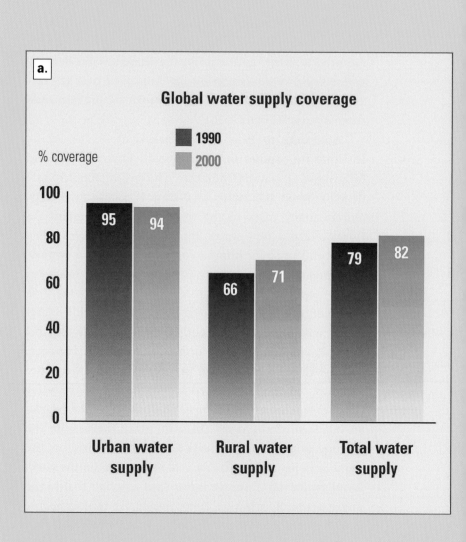

Figure 8.2 Although both the water supply and sanitation coverage have improved in rural areas, much still needs to be done to prevent such diseases as typhoid fever, which can be

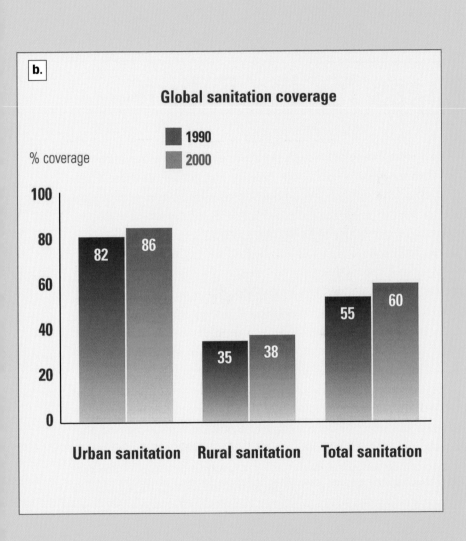

b.

Global sanitation coverage

% coverage

■ 1990
■ 2000

Urban sanitation   Rural sanitation   Total sanitation

transmitted through contaminated drinking water. More than
1 billion people in parts of Africa, Asia, and South America
still lack a clean water supply.

9

Hopes for the Future

In recent years, the ability to analyze genetic information within organisms has led to new discoveries about how the organisms function. These discoveries have, in turn, encouraged development of new treatment regimes against these organisms. A few examples of how genetic analysis can aid in the fight against typhoid fever are described in this chapter.

DISABLING WEAPONS OF BACTERIA

In May 1999, researchers announced that they had found a way to prevent a number of bacteria from causing disease. It is hoped that the findings, published in the journal *Science*, can be used to develop a new generation of vaccines and antibiotics.

Dr. Michael J. Mahan (Figure 9.1), graduate student Douglas M. Heithoff, and professors Robert L. Sinsheimer and David A. Low, from the University of California at Santa Barbara, reported that they had identified a "master switch" that controls the production of many chemicals that bacteria use to cause infection. When they knock out the switch, the bacteria are no longer capable of causing disease. The findings were published in the May 7, 2003, issue of the journal *Science*.

It seems that the master switch for **pathogenic** bacteria, such as *Vibrio cholerae* (cholera), *Yersinia* (plague), *Salmonella* (typhoid fever), and *Shigella* (dysentery) is the same. Treatment of these bacterial infections, as well as others, may be affected by this discovery. "When it comes to bacterial disease, the wake-up call has been sounded," said Mahan. It is also hoped that this discovery can be

Figure 9.1 Dr. Michael Mahan, pictured here, has been working to disable the ability of many bacteria to cause disease. This has been done through studies of the **genomes** of many disease-causing bacteria. Hopefully, this will allow us to better treat some diseases.

used in the fight against newly emerging, drug-resistant pathogens.

Mahan and his colleagues used a mutated strain of *Salmonella* with the master switch always on. This feature allows researchers to discover all of the tricks the organisms use for getting past the stomach and intestines and into organs and tissues. Mahan states that: "This has two important consequences. The bacteria are completely disabled in their ability to cause disease and these crippled bacteria work as a vaccine since they stimulate immune defenses to defend against subsequent infections."[9]

EXPANDING THE GENETIC PICTURE

In October 2001, a team of scientists from Britain, Denmark, and Vietnam reportedly deciphered the genetic code of the bacterium responsible for typhoid fever, *Salmonella typhi.* The research team worked with a strain of *Salmonella typhi* known as "CT18." This strain is resistant to all inexpensive and easily available antibiotics and may become untreatable if new antibiotics do not become available soon. Scientists are using the new genetic information to design new drugs. These drugs will be used to combat the disease and to increase our understanding of the **epidemiology** of the bacteria. Epidemiology is the study of how organisms spread into and within communities, and looks at the mechanisms that allow these organisms to cause disease.

Professor Gordon Dougan of Imperial College in London, England, one of the leaders of the English team funded by the Wellcome Trust, said: "The genetic blueprint of *Salmonella* is already leading to new methods of treatment and control, and better diagnostic tests. It provides enormous amounts of information and clues as to how it causes disease and spreads in the environment and food chain."[10]

"By studying such a lethal strain of *Salmonella*, this research also has major implications for public health threats beyond typhoid, because it is an ideal model for the evolution of drug resistance in many diseases." said Dougan in a press release.

One of the interesting details discovered by the team relates to a group of genes the researchers are calling "pseudogenes." These pseudogenes contain sequences of genetic information that are very similar to working genes but do not seem to have a function in the organism. Analysis of the pseudogenes suggests that the organism is probably limited to a single host, namely humans.

"We now know that typhoid emerged only once in human history, at some time in the last 20,000 years, most likely during early settlements. Because there is no animal reservoir for typhoid, if we can eliminate it from humans it would likely eradicate the disease altogether as typhoid could not emerge from other *Salmonella* easily," said Professor Dougan.

NARROWING THE FOCUS

In June 2002, researchers at the Institute of Food Research in Norwich, England, and the Karolinska Institute in Sweden reported that they found that changing a single base pair in one *Salmonella* gene determines if the bacteria cause short-term illness or a long-term carrier state. Previously, the factors that cause long-term or chronic infections were unclear. In a paper published in the *Proceedings of the National Academy of Sciences*, June 2002, the authors explained how they discovered the striking change in infectivity while investigating a mutant strain that produces persistent infection in mice.

The scientists found a single base change in the gene coding for the enzyme polynucleotide phosphorylase (PNPase). This enzyme normally reduces production of virulence factors. The mutant enzyme is less active, which allows increased production of virulence factors thus leading to persistent infection.

Dr. Jay Hinton of the Institute of Food Research said: "This is a new mechanism for controlling the expression of *Salmonella* virulence factors, and it's the first time that this type of gene regulation has been linked with the carrier state of typhoid."

USING OUR CURRENT KNOWLEDGE

A new combination vaccine called ViATIM was developed to provide protection against both hepatitis A and typhoid fever. The new vaccine is a combination of two well-known vaccines, Typhim Vi for typhoid fever and Avaxim for hepatitis A. It provides a rapid means of protection (14 days) for travelers who have waited until the last minute to be vaccinated. It is particularly useful when traveling in countries where both diseases are endemic.

Protection against typhoid fever lasts for three years, while protection against hepatitis A is good for up to ten years if a booster is given within six to twelve months of the initial injection. The technology involved in the vaccine keeps the two chemicals separate until just before vaccination, when they are mixed.

UNUSUAL ASSOCIATIONS

In an ironic twist, a report from the *Proceedings of the National Academy of Sciences* on March 4, 2003, entitled "Bacterial Enterotoxins are Associated with Resistance to Colon Cancer," showed that developing countries with a high rate of water-borne diseases had the lowest rate of colorectal cancer. The research, reported by G.M. Pitari et al., indicated that a bacterial enterotoxin, produced by many bacteria, binds to a receptor site found only on the surface of intestinal epithelial cells. When the enterotoxin binds to the receptor site, a series of reactions occur that cause calcium to move into the cell. This calcium introduction sets off another series of chemical reactions that confer resistance to colon cancer as reported in the March 24, 2003 issue of *The Scientist.*

In May 1998, reports began to circulate suggesting that individuals who have the mutated genes responsible for causing the disease cystic fibrosis are protected against typhoid fever. The study was supported by the National Institutes of Health/National Institute of Allergy and

Infectious Diseases and demonstrates how research in one area may lead to opportunities for applied research in other areas. Cystic fibrosis requires that a pair of genes, one from the father and one from the mother, be mutated. If only one copy of the gene is mutated and the other is normal, then the individual is a carrier of the disease. Prior to the 1950s, survival beyond the age of two for patients with cystic fibrosis was unlikely. Today, survivors average about 30 years of age before they succumb to the disease.

When a genetic disease causes death in childhood, the disease often dies out in the population—unless there is some advantage to having a mutated gene. The gene in question is known as *cftr* and codes for a protein that allows for proper movement of chloride ions. The protein's shape also serves as a receptor for attachment by various bacteria such as *Pseudomonas aeruginosa* and *Salmonella typhi*. Normally, an individual with nonmutant *cftr* genes is able to attach and engulf *Pseudomonas* and *Salmonella* bacteria. When a gene is mutated, the *Pseudomonas* is not ingested and is able to colonize the lungs and grow in layers called **biofilms**.

In the case of *Salmonella typhi*, these receptor proteins are also found on the epithelial cells of the intestines. "Uptake and ingestion of *S. typhi* by epithelial cells is part of the body's normal protective response," explains Dr. Gerald Pier, leader of the research team in a 1998 article on the Doctor's Guide to the Internet website entitled "Cystic Fibrosis Gene Protects Against Typhoid Fever."[11] "Epithelial cells ingest the bacterium and then slough off the epithelial surface. New epithelial cells soon take their place. At low concentrations of *Salmonella typhi*, this process prevents infections. High concentrations, however, can overwhelm this protective response. After *Salmonella typhi*-ingesting epithelial cells have been shed from the epithelial surface, any excess *Salmonella typhi* are free to attack the underlying tissue, which lacks this defense mechanism." A mutated form of the receptor would not allow *Salmonella typhi* to bind to the surface of the intestinal cells and, thus, carriers of mutant genes would be protected from the infection and the subsequent high mortality rate associated with the attack.

While Dr. Pier's hypothesis is suggestive, it still needs to be tested. Dr. Michael Swift of the New York Medical Center suggests that it will be necessary to determine whether people with one mutated gene copy are less susceptible to typhoid fever than those with two normal copies of the gene. The research may have had another unexpected outcome because it brought to light the role of biofilms, the unique joining and communicating in which many bacteria engage. We will explore the role of biofilms in the development of typhoid fever next.

HER GALLSTONES MADE HER DO IT

Typhoid Mary and other healthy carriers may share a strange characteristic. They all seem to have developed gallstones. Dr. Angela Prouty of the Texas Health Science Center in San Antonio found that infecting sterile gallstones with *Salmonella typhi* resulted in a tough biofilm developing over the surface of the gallstones. Bacteria bind tightly to each other and to their surface in a biofilm. This makes it difficult to wash away the bacteria from the surface. Prouty found that bile was also necessary to induce the biofilm formation. Since bile drains from the gallbladder into the lower intestine to aid in digestion, an avenue for bacterial shedding back into the environment is now present. Prouty suggested that even if antibiotics had been available to Mary, they would have been of little use since they usually do not break up biofilms. Because current antibiotics are designed to work against rapidly growing and dividing cells, they are relatively ineffective against biofilms since the organisms are in a state of semi-dormancy. Scientists are trying to develop new chemical agents that will interfere with the ability of the cells in a biofilm to communicate with each other. Until then, "The only way to get rid of the bacteria is to get rid of the gallbladder," Prouty stated at the 2001 General Meeting of the American Society for Microbiology.[12]

IS THE WATER SAFE TO DRINK?

Statistics from the CDC suggest that more than two million people around the world die annually from diseases associated with contaminated drinking water. To help change that reality, the CDC created a simple apparatus called the Safe Water System, which has been tested in Bolivia and Zambia, and has now been expanded into Kenya and Madagascar (Figure 9.2).

The disinfecting system works by creating chlorine, as sodium hypochlorite, by passing an electrical current through salt water. Funding to help produce and market the solar-powered chlorine generators has come from varied sources including United States Rotary Clubs, Proctor & Gamble, the Pan American Health Organization, and a $500,000 grant from the CDC Foundation's CARE-CDC Collaborative Health Initiative (CCHI). The overall intent of the program is to help people understand the benefits of chlorination and to make clean water available and affordable.

A number of new tests are being evaluated to determine how well they will detect bacterial contamination in water supplies. Scientists working at Technion Institute of Technology in Israel have devised a new method of tracking genetic markers for bacteria in water. In essence, this test provides a genetic fingerprint for the bacteria that can be done within one to three hours and does not require highly trained personnel. Earlier identification can lead to more effective treatment within hours of taking the test.

Another scientist also using genetic markers to identify

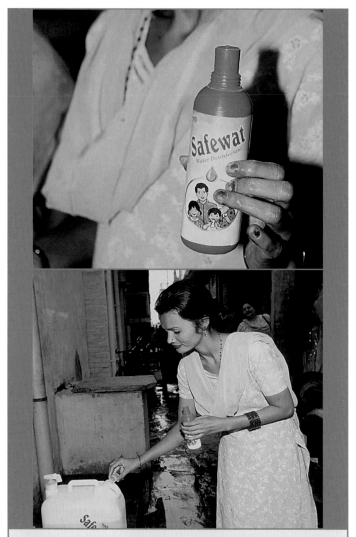

Figure 9.2 Typhoid fever is often transmitted through contaminated water. Areas that do not have toilets and wastewater treatment facilities often have this problem. The CDC and the World Health Organization (WHO) are working to combat this problem by providing people with methods to treat and clean their water. One method that has been very successful is the "Safe Water System," used in Bolivia, Zambia, Kenya, and Madagascar.

NEW USES FOR OLD CLOTHES

Another novel approach to clean drinking water involves filtering drinking water from rivers and ponds through folded pieces of cotton cloth (Figure 9.3). In India and Bangladesh, it was found that pouring water before it is consumed through a folded piece of sari (a traditional garment worn by women in these countries) at least four times would reduce cholera cases by 50%. Pore size of the threads in older saris tends to get smaller over time, making an effective filtering system. Such a system could also be effective against *Salmonella* in water supplies. Even though boiling water is the most effective way to purify it, the scarcity of wood for fuel in Bangladesh makes boiling difficult.

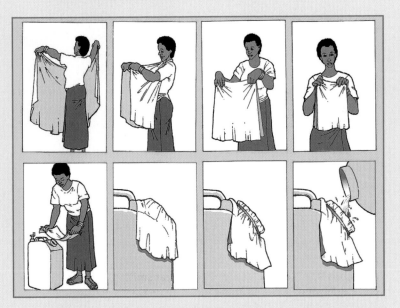

Figure 9.3 Recent studies have shown that filtering water through cloth is an effective way to get rid of harmful microorganisms. This diagram illustrates the proper way to fold the cloth and place it over the mouth of a water jug so that the water will be filtered effectively.

bacteria is Dr. Katherine Field, a microbiologist at Oregon State University. Dr. Field is currently standardizing her procedure so that a simple kit can be developed. Tests are also being developed to determine the presence of bacteria in food. Researchers are developing biological sensors (biosensors) that can detect the presence of pathogenic bacteria when foods are processed.

Biosensors are analytical devices that incorporate live organisms such as bacteria or organic molecules such as proteins to detect the presence of specific materials or molecules. They are usually connected or integrated with physical and chemical parts so that an electronic signal can be generated when the sought after activity occurs. Biosensor development at the University of Arkansas allows detection within hours. Most of the sensors created at the University of Arkansas use antibodies to trap specific bacteria. Clemson University researchers have developed nanoparticles that are luminescent and can flash an alarm if bacterial contamination is noted. Nanoparticles, because they are so small, can slip into crevices in foodstuffs that might hide a pathogen from view.

Perhaps the most intriguing new idea comes from Oregon State University. Dr. Mark Daeschel suggests that people drink a glass of Chardonnay wine with their food. This research was cited in December 2002 in the online wine journal *Fine Wine Online*.[13] Wine seems to kill bacteria in the stomach, at least in his model system. It seems that the wine's high content of malic and tartaric acids and high alcohol content kills bacteria. Other scientists remain skeptical about the work.

Whatever the new means available to detect or destroy the typhoid bacterium, it will remain a menace as long as people fail to wash their hands after a bowel movement. Those who currently have to drink contaminated water should be encouraged by the various methods that have been successfully developed by the CDC and others. However, our biggest concern will continue to be the development of healthy carriers. Only when these individuals have been identified, informed, and treated do we have a chance of finally removing typhoid fever from the list of Notifiable Diseases.

Glossary

Aerobic—Organisms that require and utilize oxygen in their cellular respiration.

AIDS—Acquired immunodeficiency syndrome; caused by a virus and characterized by loss of or diminished immune system function; death usually results from diseases such as pneumonia that would ordinarily have been taken care of by a healthy immune system.

Anaerobic—Organisms that do not and cannot use oxygen in their cellular respiration; for some organisms oxygen would be lethal.

Antibiotic—Chemical produced either by a microorganism, such as a bacteria, or a fungus, such as a mold, used to treat bacterial infections. Antibiotics are not useful in fighting viruses. Some antibiotics are currently synthesized synthetically either completely or in part, e.g., semi-synthetic penicillins such as ampicillin.

Antibiotic Resistance—Also called drug resistance; the opposite of antibiotic sensitivity. Resistant organisms such as bacteria are no longer killed or inhibited by the antibiotic.

Antibody—An immune protein or immunoglobulin; these proteins are produced by white blood cells called lymphocytes. When stimulated by a foreign protein, chemical, or cell part, lymphocytes are converted into protein (antibody) producing factories. This type of lymphocyte is known as a B lymphocyte for historical reasons.

Antigen—A molecule, group of molecules, or part of a cell that is recognized by the host immune cells as being non-self or foreign; stimulates production of antibodies (antibody generating).

Aplastic Anemia—Blood disease caused by failure of bone marrow to produce blood cells, including red and white blood cells as well as platelets.

Asymptomatic—A condition where no symptoms of the disease are shown or experienced by the patient.

Bacillus—When the term is used with a capital "B" it refers to specific genus of bacteria that have a rod-like shape. When used with the lower case "b" the term refers to the rod-like shape (a rod is longer than it is wide).

Bacteremia—The presence of live bacteria in the bloodstream. While this represents an infection, it does not necessarily imply that the bacteria can survive and reproduce in the bloodstream.

Bactericidal—Chemicals or physical conditions—e.g., temperature—that are capable of killing bacteria; e.g. antibiotics, antiseptics, and disinfectants may be bactericidal or bacteriostatic.

Bacteriostatic—Having the ability to prevent the growth or reproduction of bacteria.

Biofilm—Group of bacteria that, by living together, provides the bacteria with characteristics different from those of the individual cells. Bacteria growing in a biofilm are highly resistant to antibiotics, more resistant than the same bacteria growing as individual cells.

Carrier—Person who is infected with a disease agent but shows no outward indication of symptoms; a person who is capable of transmitting the disease organism or agent on to other patients.

Cholecystitis—Inflammation of the gallbladder which may be the result of infection in the gallbladder. Gallstones may be present.

Coccus—Bacterial cells that resemble a sphere or circle; plural is *cocci*. *Staphylococcus* (a cluster of cocci), and *streptococcus* (a chain of cocci) are common arrangements of specific groups of cocci well known for causing diseases.

DNA Relatedness—General term referring to comparisons between organisms using their DNA sequences; the greater the number of sequences that match, the closer the relationship between the organisms.

Endemic—Frequency of disease cases in a well defined geographic region where the frequency is low but there are always cases present.

Endocytosis—General term for taking other cells, particles, or molecules into the cell. Some viruses enter cells in this manner.

Endotoxin—Metabolic product released from the cell walls of gram-negative bacteria when they die. Made of lipids, polysaccharides, and peptides, they are often toxic to the cells and may cause an inflammatory reaction.

Enteric—Relating to the small intestine.

Enzyme—Protein that serves as an organic catalyst, speeding up the rate of a biochemical reaction but not consumed or used up in that reaction. All biochemical reactions within living systems are controlled or regulated by enzymes.

Glossary

Epidemic—Dramatic increase in the number of individuals showing the symptoms of a disease within a specified area, during a specified time period. In the United States, statistics to determine a true epidemic are collected and maintained by the CDC.

Epidemiology—Branch of medical science that deals with the frequency, distribution, and control of disease within a population.

Eukaryote—Organism that contains one or more cells with a nucleus and other well-developed compartments known as organelles. These organelles consist of membranes or are bounded by membranes.

Fecal-Oral Route—Transmission of microbes from fecal material to the mouth either by dirty hands and fingers or by means of food or drink contaminated with fecal materials.

Free Radical Oxygen—Reactive by-products of metabolism. Free radicals have only single electrons in their outer energy level and remove electrons from other molecules to complete their outer energy level. This electron stealing sets off a chain of biochemical events in the cells, creating instability that could destroy the cell.

Gastroenteritis—Condition in which the stomach and the intestines become inflamed. May result in nausea, vomiting, and/or diarrhea.

Genome—Sum total of all the genetic information in a cell or virus.

Gram-negative—Designation given to bacteria that have been stained by the Gram Stain Method. Gram-negative bacteria lose the color of the first or primary stain (crystal violet) and take the color of the second or counterstain (safranin—a red colored synthetic dye).

Gram-positive—Designation given to bacteria that have been stained by the Gram Stain Method. Gram-positive bacteria retain the color of the crystal violet stain and thus are colored purple to violet.

Hemagglutinin—Protein that is found as part of the outer envelope of the influenza virus; required for attachment and penetration of the virus into the cell. It is a rod-shaped spike named for its ability to cause agglutination, or clumping of red blood cells.

Haemophilus Influenzae—Bacterium found in the respiratory tract, originally thought to be responsible for the flu; causes secondary infections of the respiratory tract including pneumonia.

102

HIV — Human immunodeficiency virus; the virus responsible for AIDS.

IgG — Abbreviation for large antibody proteins called immunoglobulin G. Found in blood serum, they aid in the immune response of the body. This group includes the most common antibodies circulating in the blood.

IgM — Abbreviation for large antibody proteins called immunoglobulin M. Found in blood serum, they aid in the immune response of the body. IgM includes the antibodies that are usually produced first in response to the detection of a brand new antigen.

Infective Dose — The number of pathogenic microbes that will cause infection and visible symptoms in susceptible subjects.

Lymphatic Tissue — Lymphatic tissue includes the lymph nodes, spleen, tonsils, adenoids, and the thymus, as well as scattered patches of tissue in various area of the body such as the intestinal mesentery. Lymphatic tissue is part of the body's immune system. It produces cells that help protect the body from bacteria and other microbes.

Mesentery — Membranous tissue that attaches organs to the body wall or pieces of organs to each other.

Mononuclear Phagocyte — Type of white blood cell that is capable of engulfing bacteria, viruses, and other agents of disease. Breakdown or digestion of materials occurs within the phagocytic cell.

Neutrophil — One of the five types of white blood cells in humans. Neutrophils are the most numerous, making up about 60% of the total white blood cells under normal circumstances. They are highly phagocytic.

Organelles — "Miniature organs." Compartments within eukaryotic cells that are limited or bounded by membranes. They represent the sites of various metabolic actions and functions.

Parasite — An organism or viral particle that invades and lives within another cell or organism (called the host), using the resources of that cell. The parasite benefits from the relationship, but the host is harmed or may be killed.

Pathogenic — Organism or entity capable of causing disease.

Pediatric — Relating to children.

Glossary

Peritonitis—Inflammation of the peritoneum, which is the membrane lining the inner wall of the abdomen and pelvis. Will result in abdominal pain.

Phagocytosis—Process by which particulate material is engulfed by a cell. A type of active transport involving the entire cell.

Plasmid—Small circle of DNA outside of the bacterial chromosome; capable of self-replication, these miniature chromosomes carry a limited set of genes. They can be copied and sent by means of a protein tube from one bacterium to another, increasing the genetic variability of the recipient bacterium.

Preclinical—Studies of drugs or vaccines that are carried out in tissue, cell cultures, or animals; this phase occurs before clinical trials involving humans.

Prokaryote—Cells that lack membrane-enclosed organelles such as a nucleus. Bacteria and archaea are prokaryotic cells.

Pus—Combination of living and dead white blood cells and living and dead bacteria along with blood serum.

Rose Spots—Red to pink rash usually located on abdomen or across the trunk. Rose spots are associated with typhoid fever.

Serology—Study of the serum.

Serotype—Term that describes a microorganism that is identified by testing for the presence of specific proteins or sugars on the cell surface of that microorganism.

Serovars—New term that replaces *serotype*; refers to specific variety of microorganism that can cause antibody formation in the host.

Serum—The liquid portion of the blood that remains when the formed elements are removed.

Strains—Level of classification below the species. Specific pure cultures of bacteria are referred to as bacterial strains or isolates. Bacterial species consist of various bacterial strains that are similar but not identical to each other. Similar to the term "subspecies" in eukaryotic cells.

Subunit Vaccines—Vaccine that uses only one or more of the parts of a disease-causing organism or virus to stimulate an immune reaction.

Transduction—Means by which bacteria acquire fragments of DNA. Viruses transport DNA fragments from a donor cell to a recipient cell through transduction.

Transformation, Genetic—Alteration of the normal genetic information of cell such as a bacterium by the inclusion of additional DNA from an outside source.

Vaccine—Substance, organism, viral particle, or group of molecules that, when injected or put into the body by other means, will cause the immune system to provide an immune response to that specific agent; supplied antigens that stimulate production of antibodies.

Notes

CHAPTER 5 TREATING TYPHOID FEVER

1 "Addressing the Problem of Antimicrobial Resistance." *Emerging Infectious Diseases: A Strategy for the 21st Century.* Atlanta, Ga.: National Center for Infectious Diseases, Centers for Disease Control and Prevention. Accessed at: *www.cdc.gov/ncidod/ emergplan/antiresist.*

2 "Antimicrobial Resistance." Bethesda, Md.: Office of Communications and Public Liaison, National Institute of Allergy and Infectious Diseases, National Institutes of Health, Accessed at: *www.niaid.nih.gov/ factsheets/antimicro.htm.*

3 Tamar Nordenberg. "Miracle Drugs vs. Superbugs: Preserving The Usefulness Of Antibiotics." *FDA Consumer Magazine.* U.S. Food and Drug Administration. November–December 1998. Accessed at: *www.fda.gov/fdac/ features/1998/698_bugs.html.*

CHAPTER 6 PREVENTING TYPHOID FEVER

4 Feng Ying C. Lin et al. "The Efficacy of a *Salmonella typhi* Vi Conjugate Vaccine in Two-to-Five-Year-Old Children." *New England Journal of Medicine* 344 no. 17 (April 26, 2001): 1263–1269. Accessed at *http://content.nejm.org/ cgi/content/short/344/17/1263.*

CHAPTER 7 THE PROBLEMS OF ANTIBIOTIC RESISTANCE

5 Fact Sheet N149 available at: *http://www.who.int/inf-fs/en/ fact149.html.*

CHAPTER 8 FUTURE CONCERNS

6 *www.cbwinfo.com/Biological/ Pathogens/ST.html.*

7 Robert V. Tauxe "Emerging Foodborne Diseases: An Evolving Public Health Challenge." Emerging Infectious Diseases 3 no. 4 (October–December 1997): Accessed at *http://www.cdc.gov/ ncidod/eid/vol3no4/tauxe.htm.*

8 "FDA Warns Consumers About Frozen Mamey." *FDA Talk Paper.* Rockville, Md.: Food and Drug Administration, U.S. Department of Health and Human Services. February 20, 1999. Accessed at: *www.fda.gov/bbs/topics/ANSWERS /ANS00943.html.*

CHAPTER 9 HOPES FOR THE FUTURE

9 Douglas M. Heithoff, Robert L. Sinsheimer, David A. Low, and Michael J. Mahan. "An Essential Role for DNA Adenine Methylation in Bacterial Virulence." *Science,*Volume 284, Number 5416 (May 7, 1999): 967–970 Accessed at: *http://www.sciencedaily.com*

10 "Typhoid fever bug sequence raises hope of complete eradication." London: Imperial College. October 24, 2001. Accessed at: *www.ic.ac.uk/ templates/text_3.asp?P=3001.*

11 The Doctor's Guide to the Internet: *www.docguide.com.*

12 Clarke, Tom. "Typhoid Mary's gallstones to blame" The American Society for Microbiology General Meeting, May 23, 2001, Florida. Accessed at *www.nature.com.*

13 Fine Wine Onlline website: *www.finewineonline.co.nz.*

Bibliography

BOOKS AND ARTICLES:

Ackers, Marta-Louise, et al. "Laboratory-Based Surveillance of Salmonella Serotype Typhi Infections in the United States: Antimicrobial Resistance on the Rise." *Journal of the American Medical Association*, 283:20. (May 24, 2000): 2668–2673.

"Addressing the Problem of Antimicrobial Resistance." *Emerging Infectious Diseases: A Strategy for the 21st Century.* Atlanta, Ga.: National Center for Infectious Diseases, Centers for Disease Control and Prevention. Accessed at: *www.cdc.gov/ncidod/emergplan/antiresist.*

Alcamo, I. Edward. *Fundamentals of Microbiology*, Fifth Edition. New York: The Benjamin Cummings Publishing Company, 1997.

American Medical Association, et al. "Foodborne Illnesses Table: Bacterial Agents." January, 2001. Accessed at: *http://www.ama-assn.org.*

"Antimicrobial Resistance." Bethesda, Md.: Office of Communications and Public Liaison, National Institute of Allergy and Infectious Diseases, National Institutes of Health. June 2000. Accessed at: *www.niaid.nih.gov/factsheets/antimicro.htm.*

Aplastic Anemia and MDS International Foundation, Inc. "What are these diseases—aplastic anemia, myelodysplastic syndromes, and PNH?" Annapolis, Md.: Aplastic Anemia and MDS International Foundation, Inc., 2003. Accessed at: *http://aplastic.eyemg.com.*

Arraf, Jane. "Primate population a Perplexing Problem for New Delhi." CNN. November 18, 1999. Accessed at *http://www.cnn.com.*

Baur, John. "Test developed to Determine Source of Fecal Coliform." Oregon State University News and Communication Services. January 31, 2002. Accessed at *www.oregonstate.edu.*

Carson-DeWitt, Rosalyn S. "Typhoid Fever." Thomson Corporation. January 28, 2003. Accessed at *http://www.principalhealthnews.com.*

"Caused By Gram-Negative Bacilli: Enterobacteriaceae Infections." In *The Merck Manual of Diagnosis and Therapy*, Section 13, Chapter 157. Beers, Mark H., and Robert Berkow Robert M. Bogin, and Andrew J. Fletcher, eds. 17th ed., Centennial ed. Whitehouse Station, N.J.: Merck, 1999. Accessed at: *http://www.merck.com/pubs/mmanual.*

Chamberlain, Neal R. "Alexander the Great Died of Typhoid Fever." Suite101.com. July 10, 1998. Accessed at *http://www.suite101.com/article.cfm/251/8105.*

Bibliography

Chamberlain, Neal R. "New Vaccine Protects Children from Typhoid Fever." Suite101.com. May 11, 2001. Accessed at *http://www.suite101.com/article.cfm/251/68878.*

Clarke, Tom. "Typhoid Mary's gallstones to blame." The American Society for Microbiology General Meeting, May 23, 2001, Florida. Accessed at *www.nature.com.*

Clements, Mark O., Sofia Eriksson, Arthur Thompson, Sacha Lucchini, Jay C.D. Hinton, Staffan Normark, and Mikael Rhen. "Polynucleotide phosphorylase is a global regulator of virulence and persistency in *Salmonella enterica.*" *Proceedings of the National Academy of Science.* Vol. 99, no. 13. June 25, 2002.

Coakley, Frances, ed. *A Manx Note Book: An Electronic Compendium of Matters Past and Present Connected with the Isle of Man.* Accessed at: *www.ee.surrey.ac.uk/Contrib/manx/famhist/genealgy/diseases.htm.*

Cole, Michelle. "Wine may Prevent Food Poisoning and Kill Bacteria." Newhouse News Service. Published December 2002 at: *http://www.finewineonline.co.nz.*

Corales, Robert et al. "Typhoid Fever." *EMedicine.* July 18, 2002. Accessed at *http://www.emedicine.com.*

"Cystic Fibrosis Gene Protects Against Typhoid Fever." *The Doctor's Guide to the Internet.* May 6, 1998. Accessed at *www.docguide.com.*

"Diagnosis and management of foodborne illnesses: a primer for physicians." *MMWR Recomm. Rep. 2001* Jan 26:50 (RR–2):1–69.

"FDA Warns Consumers About Frozen Mamey." *FDA Talk Paper.* Rockville, Md.: Food and Drug Administration, U.S. Department of Health and Human Services. February 20, 1999. Accessed at: *www.fda.gov.*

Garbo, Jon. "Typhoid Fever Outbreak Identified Among MSM in Ohio." *Gay Health.* April 30, 2001. Accessed at *http://www.gayhealth.com.*

Garmony, Helen S., Katherine A. Brown, and Richard W. Titball "Salmonella Vaccines for use in Humans: Present and Future Perspectives." *FEMS Microbiology Reviews* 26, no. 4 (November 2002): 339–353.

"Genetic markers used to detect bacteria in water." Edie–The Online Community for Water, Waste, and Environmental Professionals. News Update October 5, 2002. Accessed at *www.edie.net.*

Global Water Supply and Sanitation Assessment 2000 Report, World Health Organization (WHO) and United Nations International Children's emergency Fund (UNICEF), 2000. Accessed at: *http://www.unep.org/vitalwater/18.htm.*

Heithoff, Douglas M., Robert L. Sinsheimer, David A. Low, and Michael J. Mahan. "An Essential Role for DNA Adenine Methylation in Bacterial Virulence." *Science,* Volume 284, Number 5416 (May 7, 1999): 967–970. Accessed at: *http://www.sciencedaily.com.*

Huckstep, R.L. *Typhoid Fever and Other Salmonella Infections.* Edinburgh, Scotland, and London, U.K.: E&S Livingstone Ltd.

Kapoor, S.K., G. Kumar, C.S. Pandav, and K. Anand. "Incidents of Low Birthweight in Rural Ballagbash, Haryand." Indian Pedriacs 38 (2001): 271–275. Accessed at *http://www.indianpediatrics.net/march2001/march-271-275.htm.*

Kariuki, Samuel, et al. "Genotypic Analysis of Multidrug-Resistant *Salmonella enterica* Serovar Typhi, Kenya." *Emerging Infectious Diseases* 6 no. 6 (November-December 2000): *Accessed at http://www.cdc.gov.*

Kazemifar, A.R. "Treatment of Typhoid Fever." *Shiraz E-Medical Journal.* 2000. Accessed at *http://www.sums.ac.ir/~semj/vol2/jan2001/typhoidRx.htm.*

Kidgell, Claire, Ulrike Reichard, John Wain, Bodo Linz, Mia Tordahl, Gordon Dougan, and Mark Achtman. "*Salmonella typhi,* the causative agent of typhoid fever, is approximately 50,000 years old," *Infection, Genetics and Evolution* 2, no. 1 (October 2002): 39–45.

Kirby, David. "New Resistant Gonorrhea Migrating to Mainland U.S." *New York Times,* Late Edition—Final, Section F, Page 5, Column 1. May 7, 2002.

Korbsrisate, Sunee, Ariya Thanomsakyuth, Napatawn Banchuin, Stan McKay, Moazzem Hossain, and Suttipant Sarasombath. "Characterization Of A Phase 1-D Epitope On *Salmonella Typhi* Flagellin And Its Role In The Serodiagnosis Of Typhoid Fever." Mahidol University Annual Research Abstracts 1999. Accessed at: *http://www.mahidol.ac.th/abstracts/annual1999/0208.htm.*

Kumar, Ashwani, Vineet Arora, Anu Bashamboo, and Sher Ali. "Detection of *Salmonella typhi* by polymerase chain reaction: Implications in diagnosis of typhoid fever." *Infection, Genetics and Evolution* 2, no. 2 (December 2002): 107–110.

Bibliography

Lin, Feng Ying C., et al. "The Efficacy of a *Salmonella typhi* Vi Conjugate Vaccine in Two-to-Five-Year-Old Children." *New England Journal of Medicine* 344 no. 17 (April 26, 2001): 1263–1269. Accessed at *http://content.nejm.org/cgi/content/short/344/17/1263.*

Marill, Michele Cohen. "Safe Water, Simply Made: A CDC Foundation program brings a CDC project to thousands of people." *Frontline Newsletter.* 2000. Accessed at: *http://www.cdcfoundation.org.*

Mermin, Jonathan, et al. "Typhoid Fever in the United States, 1985–1994, Changing Risks of International Travel and Increasing Microbial Resistance." *Archives of Internal Medicine* 158 no. 6 (March 23, 1998).

Miller, Fred. "Biosensors Promise Rapid Detection of Food Pathogens." University of Arkansas Department of Agriculture, Arkansas Agricultural Experiment Station. Column no. 39, April 18, 2002. Accessed at: *http://www.uark.edu/depts/agripub/Publications/Agnews/agnews02-32.html.*

"Miscellaneous Antibiotics, Chloramphenicol." *The Merck Manual of Diagnosis and Therapy,* Section 13, Chapter 153. Beers, Mark H., and Robert Berkow Robert M. Bogin, and Andrew J. Fletcher, eds. 17th ed., Centennial ed. Whitehouse Station, N.J.: Merck, 1999. Accessed at: *http://www.merck.com/pubs/mmanual.*

"Monitoring Antibiotics in Shrimp," *New York Times,* Late Edition, 3 June 2002, sec. A, p.13, Col. 3.

Murphy, Miriam B."Salt Lake City Had its Typhoid Mary." *History Blazer.* April 1996. Accessed at *http://historytogo.utah.gov.*

Nordenberg, Tamar. "Miracle Drugs vs. Superbugs: Preserving The Usefulness Of Antibiotics." *FDA Consumer Magazine.* U.S. Food and Drug Administration. (November-December 1998). Accessed at: *www.fda.gov.*

Pitari, G.M., et al., "Bacterial enterotoxins are associated with resistance to colon cancer," *Proceedings of the National Academy of Sciences* 100 (March 4, 2003): 2695–9.

Powell, Kendall. "Clothes clean drinking water." *Nature* Science Update. January 14, 2003. Accessed at *www.nature.com.*

"Quinolones and the Clinical Laboratory." Centers for Disease Control, National Center for Infectious Disease, Division of Healthcare Quality Promotion, Accessed at: *http://www.cdc.gov.*

"Researchers Create Biosensors To Protect Food And Water Supplies." Clemson University. Published at Space Daily, *http://www.spacedaily.com/news/terrorwar-02p.html.*

Singh, Bir. "Epidemiology: Typhoid fever." 2000. Accessed at: *http://www.indegene.com*

Singh, Sarman. "Treatise on Pathogenesis and Laboratory Diagnosis." New Delhi, India Department of Laboratory Medicine, All India Institute of Medical Sciences. Accessed at: *http://www.indegene.com/Gen/FeatArt/indGenFeatArt13child3.html.*

Skipton, Sharon and Bruce Dvorak. "Drinking Water: Chloramines Water Disinfection in Omaha Metropolitan Utilities District." Nebraska Cooperative Extension NF02-505. Accessed at: *http://www.ianr.unl.edu/pubs/water/nf505.htm.*

"Surveillance and Reporting Guidelines for Typhoid." Shoreline, Wash.: Office of Epidemiology, Washington State Department of Health. Accessed at: *http://www.doh.wa.gov.*

Tauxe, Robert V. "Emerging Foodborne Diseases: An Evolving Public Health Challenge." Emerging Infectious Diseases 3 no. 4 (October-December 1997): Accessed at *http://www.cdc.gov/ncidod/eid/vol3no4/tauxe.htm.*

Tritz, Gerald J. "Invasive Gastroenteritis." Lecture at Kirksville College of Osteopathic Medicine, Kirksville, Mo. October 8, 1999. Accessed at: *http://www.kcom.edu/faculty/chamberlain/Website/tritzid/shigello.htm.*

"Typhoid big problem in poor countries." *Dawn the Internet Edition.* February 7, 2002. Accessed at *http://www.dawn.com/2002/02/07/nat20.htm.*

"Typhoid fever bug sequence raises hope of complete eradication." London: Imperial College. October 24, 2001. Accessed at: *www.ic.ac.uk.*

"Typhoid Fever: essential data." Fact sheets on Chemical and Biological Warfare Agents, Version 2.1. September 2002, Accessed at: *http://www.cbwinfo.com.*

"Typhoid Fever in the United States." National Institute of Child Health and Human Development, April 25, 2001. Accessed at: *http://www.nichd.nih.gov.*

Bibliography

WEB RESOURCES:

Aventis Pasteur, information about Typhoid Fever and its vaccine
www.aventispasteur.com/us/vaccines/geneinfo4.html.

All India Institute, *www.aiims.ac.in/new_page_4.htm.*

History and Background Information about Chloramphenicol,
www.marvistavet.com/html/body_chloramphenicol.html.

History of the Chicago River, *www.inficad.com/~ksup/chiriver.html.*

History of Typhoid Fever, *www.geocities.com/avinash_abhyankar/history.htm.*

Lasker Foundation, Albert Lasker Award for Clinical Research,
www.laskerfoundation.org/awards/library/1962clinical.shtml.

National University of Ireland, Galway. Information about Gastrointestinal
Infections, *www.nuigalway.ie/bac/Gastrointestinal_Infection.html.*

"New Hepatitis A/Typhoid Fever Combination Vaccine, ViATIM, Launched
in England." Doctor's Guide to the Internet, Global Addition. Accessed at:
www.pslgroup.com/dg/207A0A.htm.

Office of Educational Programs, NASA Glenn Research Center, "Reliving the
Wright Way: Biography of Wilbur Wright," *wright.nasa.gov/wilbur.htm.*

Rutgers History Department, Rutgers University. Information about
Military Medicine and the Spanish-American War,
history.rutgers.edu/graduate/ab02ciri.htm.

Sotos, John. "The Medical History of President Zachary Taylor."
Accessed at: *www.doctorzebra.com/prez/g12.htm.*

Travel Information from Travelite (India),
http://www.traveliteindia.com/guide/visa.htm.

World Health Organization, Information about Typhoid Fever,
www.who.int/inf-fs/en/fact149.html.

Websites

Centers for Disease Control and Prevention
www.cdc.gov

World Health Organization
www.who.int

National Institutes of Health
www.nih.gov

MedlinePlus Health Information (United States National Library of Medicine and National Institutes of Health)
www.medlineplus.gov

WebMD
www.webmd.com

Index

Index

Index

HIV. *See* Human immuno-
deficiency virus
host immune cell, 24, 29,
91, 100, 105–6
Human immunodeficien-
cy virus (HIV), 58,
103

immune system, 21–22,
24, 26, 44, 46, 53, 60,
90, 100, 104, 106–7
immunoglobulin, 100
IgG, 45, 104
IgM, 45, 104
infectious diseases, 6, 28
infectious dose, 42, 48,
104
influenza, 6, 32, 67, 103,
107
Institute of Food
Research, 91
International Symposium
on Typhoid Fever and
Other Salmonelloses,
81
International Vaccine
Institute, 81
intestine, 67, 102, 104
infections of, 19, 26,
28, 42, 84, 90

Jamestown, Virginia
deaths by typhoid
fever in, 10
Japanese encephalitis, 32
Jenner, Edward
and smallpox vaccine,
9
*Journal of the American
Medical Association,*
73

Kolle, Wilhelm
and typhoid vaccine,
14

Labella, Tony
carrier of typhoid
fever, 13
Legionnaires disease, 6
lipid, 102
liver, 26, 28, 50
Low, David A.
research of, 88
Lyme disease, 6, 32
lymphatic tissue, 26, 28,
104
lymph nodes, 26, 42, 104
lysosome, 20

Mahan, Michael J.
research of, 88–90
malaria, 6–7, 34, 37–38,
58, 60, 73
Mallon, Mary (Typhoid
Mary)
carrier of typhoid
fever, 10–13, 49, 94
measles, 31–32
meningitis, 6, 60
Meningococcal menin-
gitis, 32
mesentery, 28, 42, 104
metabolism, 103
Metropolitan Sanitary
District of Greater
Chicago, 14
microbe, 44, 58, 66, 70,
72, 103–4
microorganism, 18, 44,
66–68, 100, 106
microscope
invention of, 7
mitochondria, 20
MMR, 32
mononuclear phagocyte,
26, 104
*Morbidity and Mortality
Weekly Report,* 37, 47
Musa, Antonius
and typhoid fever, 8

National Institute of
Allergy and Infectious
Diseases (NIAID),
72–73, 92–93
National Institute of
Child Health and
Development
(NICHD), 59, 74
National Institutes of
Health (NIH), 55–56,
59, 72, 74, 92–93
neutrophil, 26, 105
*New England Journal of
Medicine,* 59
New York Times, 67, 76
NIAID. *See* National
Institute of Allergy
and Infectious
Diseases
NICHD. *See* National
Institute of Child
Health and
Development
NIH. *See* National
Institutes of Health
Notifiable Bacterial Food-
borne Disease or
Condition, 36, 99
nucleus, 20–21, 103, 106

organelles, 20–21, 103,
105–6

Pang, Tikki
research of, 81
parasite, 105
paratyphoid fever, 49, 62
Parry, Chris
research of, 81
pathogenic, 88, 105
pediatric, 105
penicillin, 22, 50, 66, 72,
100
peptide, 102
peptidoglycan, 21–22, 24

Picture Credits

About the Author

Dr. Donald Emmeluth spent most of his teaching career in upstate New York. An avid hiker and golfer, both endeavors provided him with ample opportunities to view the forests and grasslands of the countryside. In 1999, Dr. Emmeluth retired from the State University of New York system and moved to the warmer climate of Savannah, Georgia. He became a member of the Biology Department of Armstrong Atlantic State University (AASU) in Savannah. He continues to hike after golf balls on the various courses in and around Savannah and the Hilton Head, South Carolina, areas.

At AASU, Dr. Emmeluth teaches a course entitled Principles of Biology, Microbiology, Microorganisms, and Disease as well as a bioethics module that is part of the ethics course on campus. He developed and maintains the Biology Department website. Dr. Emmeluth has also published several journal articles and is the co-author of a high school biology textbook. His most recent article appeared in the February 2002 issue of *The American Biology Teacher*. The topic was bioinformatics. He has also authored another of the books in this series about Influenza. He has served as President of the National Association of Biology Teachers. During his career, Dr. Emmeluth has received a number of honors and awards including the Chancellor's Award for Excellence in Teaching and the Two-Year College Biology Teaching Award from NABT.

About the Editor

The late I. Edward Alcamo was a Distinguished Teaching Professor of Microbiology at the State University of New York at Farmingdale. Alcamo studied biology at Iona College in New York and earned his M.S. and Ph.D. degrees in microbiology at St. John's University, also in New York. He taught at Farmingdale for over 30 years. In 2000, Alcamo won the Carski Award for Distinguished Teaching in Microbiology, the highest honor for microbiology teachers in the United States. He was a member of the American Society for Microbiology, the National Association of Biology Teachers, and the American Medical Writers Association. Alcamo authored numerous books on the subjects of microbiology, AIDS, and DNA technology as well as the award-winning textbook *Fundamentals of Microbiology*, now in its sixth edition.